ANTHEM GUIDE TO ESSAY WRITING

ANTHEM GUIDE TO ESSAY WRITING

CAROLE L. HAMILTON

ANTHEM PRESS
LONDON · NEW YORK · DELHI

Anthem Press
An imprint of Wimbledon Publishing Company
www.anthempress.com

This edition first published in UK and USA 2011
by ANTHEM PRESS
75-76 Blackfriars Road, London SE1 8HA, UK
or PO Box 9779, London SW19 7ZG, UK
and
244 Madison Ave. #116, New York, NY 10016, USA

British Library Cataloguing in Publication Data
A catalogue record for this book is available from the British Library.

Library of Congress Cataloging-in-Publication Data
Hamilton, Carole L., 1951-
Anthem guide to essay writing / Carole L. Hamilton.
                    p. cm.
Includes bibliographical references and index.
ISBN 978-0-85728-975-9 (pbk. : alk. paper)
1. Essay–Authorship–Handbooks, manuals, etc. 2. English language–Rhetoric–
Handbooks, manuals, etc. I. Title. II. Title: Guide to essay writing.
PN4500.H25 2011
808.4–dc22
                    2011014784

ISBN-13: 978 0 85728 975 9 (Pbk)
ISBN-10: 0 85728 975 6 (Pbk)

This title is also available as an eBook.

CONTENTS

INTRODUCTION

How do writers find a state of mind where words flow and ideas are fully explored? In my classroom, I can observe the various ways in which my students achieve (or do not achieve) this state, thanks to a software product that displays their screens on my computer as they write. Without intruding on their concentration, I can watch how they work, which gives me a window into their writing state of mind. A mere ten minutes after beginning, one student has an outline open, plus a page of relevant quotations, and a half-written introduction on her screen. What she has written is not terribly exciting, but she is focused and working productively. Another student is flipping through her notes, a blank document open on her screen. Half an hour later, only one sentence has been written. On another screen, a phrase is deleted, rewritten, deleted, and written again. Each student has a different writing obstacle. One has not read carefully enough, one needs to organize better, one should have spent more time brainstorming ideas so that she could approach the task with more confidence. I will select an appropriate method to help each student find a more productive way to write.

If your experience mirrors my students' difficulties in getting started, staying on task, or developing an essay that you are proud to turn in, you will find some useful suggestions in this book, though there is no need to adopt every one of them. You will find here guidelines for most kinds of essays and most classes, from secondary school through university classes, from history and English to politics and government and the natural sciences. I hope that my years of observing and guiding young writers has resulted in a handbook that will help you find your flow state of writing more easily, so you can write bold, eloquent essays with confidence and enjoyment.

Carole Hamilton, 2011

Thank you to those who contributed sample essays for this book: former students Amelia, Caleb, Cyndell, Haleigh, Haley, Lila, and Rim; my colleague E. Palmer Seeley; and my daughter, Aubrey Hamilton.

READING AND RESEARCHING

1.1 Annotating Texts

In old black-and-white films, the young newspaper writer tilts his hat off his forehead, puts a clean sheet of paper into a manual typewriter, and starts writing the lead article that will hit the front page the next day. The paragraphs flow from his razor-sharp mind straight to the paper, in a well ordered march of ideas. But, as they say, "life ain't like the movies." Nor is writing. A good essay doesn't spring to the mind immediately, but evolves slowly, after hard thinking and planning. It starts with making keen observations of the material under study. That is why this book on *writing* starts with training your eye in *reading*. This chapter teaches you one surefire way to annotate a text, identifying passages and ideas that are worth writing about. You will develop your own method as you become a more experienced close reader.

No matter what you are annotating, whether scholarly articles, poetry, fiction, art, charts, or statistical data, read with pen or stylus in hand, ready to highlight things that are unusual, interesting, puzzling, or surprising. Pick texts that are within your grasp—not highly complex, jargon-filled material—and then spend the time to truly understand them. Don't skip over the parts that confuse you. They may contain the "keys to the kingdom" of understanding the piece, even if they don't proffer their wisdom at once. Write a question mark or tentative interpretation next to the difficult parts, and come back to them later. Also gloss difficult words or phrases, guessing at the meaning from the context. Write this meaning in the margin and look it up later for confirmation or correction. Marginal notes can also include quick summaries, your immediate reaction, questions, connections to other materials. Highlight key examples, statistics, analogies, rhetorical devices, and so on. Also note the writer's tone and point of view. Your eventual goal is to read quickly and efficiently, making margin notes while sustaining your attention to the unfolding story. However, until you reach a level of confident proficiency, work slowly so that you discover key passages that will take your analysis beyond the obvious to an interpretation that you will enjoy explaining.

Judge how much to annotate so that you don't underline every line or get so bogged down that you lose the thread of meaning. If this occurs, read once quickly for meaning, just highlighting what stands out the most as you go, then re-read, catching deeper nuances in the second pass.

You can also create an index of passages electronically or inside the front cover of your book, so that you can easily find the interesting passages, organized by topic. This method is especially helpful for longer texts. Train yourself to update your index as you read. You may think that you will remember a given incident, but most likely, you won't. Some new idea will emerge and the previous one will be lost. So get it down now, and you will save hours of frustration when you write your essay. Sample index:

The Things They Carried (inside cover)

Games 32, 37, 70
Definitions of war 80, 85
Appositives 7, 9, 15, 17, 22, 34, 39, 43, 45, 45, 51
Storytelling 32, 34, 39, 72, 77, 78, 86, 106, 112, 127, 130, 236
Truth 46, 71, 77, 82, 85, 89, 89, 180

You can see how an index you make can save you much time when looking for passages to support your essay.

What to highlight:

- Main ideas and themes

- Ambiguous/puzzling words, phrases, imagery

- Core concepts, phrases, and themes

- Poetic devices or rhetorical devices

- Useful analogies, examples, and recurring motifs

- Shifts in mood, pace, topic, point of view, plot, relationships

- Key statistics, significant quotations, potential evidence

- Writer's tone and point of view

What to jot in the margins:

- Meanings/definitions

- Reactions, questions, interpretations

- Brief summary of action or ideas

Sample Annotation of a Poem:

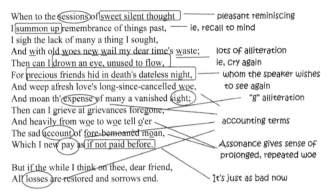

Sonnet 30 by William Shakespeare

When to the sessions of sweet silent thought ——— pleasant reminiscing
I summon up remembrance of things past, —— ie, recall to mind
I sigh the lack of many a thing I sought,
And with old woes new wail my dear time's waste; lots of alliteration
Then can I drown an eye, unused to flow, ie, cry again
For precious friends hid in death's dateless night, ——— whom the speaker wishes
And weep afresh love's long-since-cancelled woe, to see again
And moan th'expense of many a vanished sight; "g" alliteration
Then can I grieve at grievances foregone,
And heavily from woe to woe tell o'er — accounting terms
The sad account of fore-bemoaned moan,
Which I new pay as if not paid before. Assonance gives sense of
prolonged, repeated woe
But if the while I think on thee, dear friend,
All losses are restored and sorrows end. It's just as bad now

There is no specific way to annotate. Find a method that works for you. Make sure that your abbreviations will make sense to you later! You can also insert page tabs to make it easy to find a specific page. There is no need to annotate every paragraph or page, for that will require you to sort through more information than you might need.

Sample Annotation of Research Material:

156 POWER TRIP

noting my gag reflex, "but you get used to it." I grew ever warier when he warned me not to touch any of the liquid nitrogen dripping from the tank because it could give me second-degree burns. It was hard for me to believe that this putrid stuff could possibly have life-giving properties. But I learned that a plant with no nitrogen is like a computer with no cord—without nitrogen the plant cannot "turn on," so to speak. Nitrogen is a primary element in chlorophyll—the pigment that gives plants their green color and enables them to channel energy from sunlight into the creation of the fibers and sugars that make them a source of nourishment.

Maneuvering a tractor through a cornfield is a little like steering a ship through waves—it's hard to keep the vessel in a straight line on the sloping, bumpy earth and then to repeat that straight line exactly as you traverse the rest of the field, without overlapping any areas on which you've already sprayed nitrogen. Conventional tractors routinely overlap on fertilizer application, wasting precious resources. Ken is able to overcome this costly human error because his tractor drives itself. "See the GPS system," Nick asked, pointing to a small round blinking device on the dashboard. That device was feeding signals to a satellite monitoring the position of the tractor on the field. The satellite was then automatically feeding those location coordinates into an autopilot system that steers the tractor on a precise course, never double-applying fertilizer to the same patch of soil.

Efficiency

Precision COOKING OIL 157

farms actually go to waste because they're blindly doused on areas of soil that in fact have sufficient levels of nitrogen. Other agriculture experts I interviewed put that number even higher, saying that up to 35 percent of the nitrogen typically sprayed on farmland goes to waste, draining out of the soil and polluting nearby bodies of water.

Precision fertilizer application technologies are not yet in widespread use—only about 5 to 10 percent of American farmers have fully adopted them—but they hold promise. The software has shaved down Ken's fertilizer applications by nearly 15 percent, and he expects the savings to increase as the technology evolves and he adapts to using it. Ken also plants genetically modified corn seeds known as No. 6169, engineered by Monsanto to have built-in characteristics that enable the plant to repel insects, for instance, and withstand herbicides (so that products such as Roundup can be sprayed directly on the crops, "killing everything but the corn," as he explained it). The seeds will soon be engineered to utilize nitrogen fertilizers more efficiently than conventional seeds—an innovation that will further trim fertilizer use. "We are using 10 percent less fertilizer today than we were a decade ago," Ken said, "and in that time our yields have nearly doubled."

Those are crucial gains, he told me, at a time of unstable energy prices. As natural gas and oil prices surged in recent years, the costs of fertilizers nearly quadrupled. In 2005, when natural gas prices were low, a 2.2-ton tank of anhydrous ammonia cost under $400. When gas prices

Engineered seeds

1.2   Taking Notes

Computers make it easy to grab a bit of text and save it for easy insertion into an essay. Perhaps the phrase "note-taking" should be replaced by "source-snipping." Because it is so easy, you can be tempted to save every possible passage, thus creating a mass of material to sort through later. This only delays the thinking time needed to identify the specific quotations that are relevant and useful to keep. So take the time to select brief passages that state an idea concisely. Include your reactions as you go, being careful to distinguish your words from source material. Use discretion in selecting each passage, but go ahead and record passages you think you might need it, as they may be difficult to find later.

If you take notes on a computer, consider one of the many programs that allow you to replicate note cards. These programs make it easy to move the cards around when you get ready to organize your essay.

During the note-taking phase make sure that you clearly differentiate between paraphrased material, quoted words, and your own observations. To keep track of which words are yours and which come from others, put quotation marks around all words taken directly from the source, and write the author and page number after each paragraph. For paraphrased material, leave out the quotation marks, but, again, put the author and page number after the paraphrased material. Put the ideas into your own words, but be sure to preserve the original sense. Put [brackets] around all of your own comments, or type them in a different font, or use some other means to make them stand out from notes from sources. Taking the time to identify every single line of notes will save you hours of frustration later. It is very difficult to find a particular passage again when you do not have the page number or, worse, cannot remember which source contained it.

For research essays, write the full citation at the top of each page of notes, along with a one-sentence summary of the content of this source. If you happen to have an idea of what subtopics you will need, you can start a page of notes for each one, making sure to include a citation for each piece of quoted evidence. Start your works cited page immediately and keep it current as you proceed. Keep your working thesis literally in front of you as you read; otherwise, you may find yourself wasting time on irrelevant though interesting reading. Start a draft outline as soon as the structure of the essay begins to take shape in your mind. Revise the outline and thesis as you go.

Sample Note for an Essay on Cuba:

Notes from Nelson Amaro Victoria "Mass and Class in the Origins of the Cuban Revolution" *Studies in Comparative International Development* **(SCID) Vol 4 Number 10 October 1968 pgs 223-237 EBSCO Dec 18, 2009**

"From 1954 to 1959, 82.3 percent [of rural peasants] migrated to urban areas [looking for work in the burgeoning industries, but most of them became the] urban unemployed." Victoria 224

"69 percent" of the urban unemployed "expected [Cuba's] economic problems to be resolved politically." Victoria 225

"Zeitlin's (1966b: 47ff.) study confirms…that the greater degree of marginality of industrial workers to positions of authority, the greater their support of the Revolution. Further, workers employed for longer periods of time were less likely to support the Revolution than were the underemployed and unemployed." Victoria 225 [Marxism targets wage earners and proceeds from the ground up. Is this what occurred in Cuba?]

"Practically all the Cuban people identified with the 26th of July Movement, and it in turn tried by every means to disseminate its ideological content as widely as possible." Victoria 230 [note how many tvs the people had—this was a media event]

"The people continued to be elated. Castro spoke practically every week on television, and was followed in his travels by representatives of all the media. His speeches were often made without warning, and lasted for many hours, upsetting the usual schedule of programs. Those in power were constantly in the news and the country was being rocked by the ongoing changes: the Rent Laws, the Agrarian Reform, the Tax Reform, the military trials of those accused of committing genocide during the Batista regime; the efforts of the various revolutionary organizations." Victoria 231 [were these Castro's reforms? If so, they would certainly make the low wage earners happy]

"'People's Shops' were established, which offered merchandise to the peasants at practically cost price. The Prime Minister himself took walks in these zones, and it was rumored that he carried a checkbook and would distribute checks then and there, according to the needs of the various zones." Victoria 231 [he's making himself into a hero of the people, erasing the bureaucracy between the president and his citizens]

"The Cuban Revolution underwent an essential change in its nature; the intervening factor was a modification in the thoughts expressed by the principal leaders… [Castro mentioned] "dangers suffered by Cuba due to the existence of 'Yankee Imperialism' and of the old social classes which had reigned over Cuba." Victoria 235

There was a "lack of faith in the political institutions." Victoria 236

Notice that the student has put each paragraph into quotation marks and added the author name and page number after it. His own words are in brackets. When he begins to insert material from this source into his essay, he will be less likely to inadvertently present the source information as his own words. The full citation is at the top of the page, making it easy to prepare the works cited list, too.

Summing Up

Keep careful track of the sources of your research material, appending each passage with the citation. Start your bibliography immediately and develop a consistent system of distinguishing your own comments from the words you are quoting or paraphrasing. Use discretion in selecting passages, so that you do not simply delay the sorting process until later, but include anything that you might use.

2

GENERATING IDEAS

2.1 Introduction

Generating ideas from your source material is the most creative, most fun part of writing an essay. Part close observation, part connecting the dots, this critical thinking stage engages activities that our pattern-finding brains find intrinsically interesting and rewarding. It requires both divergent thinking (generating many ideas and connections) and convergent thinking (focusing on a solution) to explore the range of possibilities and then to synthesize them to discover how the parts add up to more than the whole. It starts with making alert observations of concrete, undeniable, facts and truths about a text or topic. And it can help you arrive at a thesis that is often as complex and artful as the original text being analyzed. So allow plenty of time to enjoy the process.

Samuel Johnson said that "What is written without effort is read without pleasure." In other words, you cannot add anything new to a topic if all you do is amass found data into an ordered procession. Instead, think beyond and through the information to discover new implications—making inferences, accounting for context, piecing together disparate bits of evidence, noticing patterns, and drawing conclusions. Consider also what is not stated, and what underlying assumptions exist, as well as implications and consequences. Derive a working thesis and then test it by sifting through your materials for supporting and counter-evidence. You will expand your ideas when you do some free-writing to figure out what you think. All good thinkers think with a pen (or keyboard). See Chapter 3.1 on how to free-write.

2.2   For Literature Essays

Good fiction draws you into its world and makes you forget that you are reading. This creates a problem, though, because such reading is passive—you can lose the critical distance necessary to analyze *how* the piece drew you in, *how* it made you feel that its world is palpable and logical. If everyone had time to read literature twice through, once for enjoyment and once to look at it critically, analyzing literature would be a simple affair. But chances are that you don't have time to re-read assignments, so tuning your ability to notice the writer's craft as you read will not only make for a better analytical essay, it will increase your enjoyment, too. As you read, consider the deeper issues of character motivation, social context, the philosophical ideas underlying the text, and the events or ideas that are left out, as well as how the writing itself contributes to the meaning. This entails slowing down, but not to the point that you lose track of the main ideas of the text.

The goal of a literature essay is to derive your own theory about the work, to develop your ideas fully enough that a skeptical reader can be convinced, and to support your claims with many succinct and vivid quotations from the text. Usually you do not want to quote long blocks of the text, but if you do want to include a longer passage, make sure to balance it with equal commentary of your own about what it means.

Don't make the common mistake of equating the narrator with the writer. In fact, the narrator may represent a position that the writer considers reprehensible. Sometimes the author creates a narrator that serves as a puppet, presenting a viewpoint designed to provoke you into disagreement, which nudges you closer to the author's thinking. One hint of this possibility might come through the writer's tone, which may be arch, sarcastic, or falsely approving. Often there seems to be no "tone" at all—that the writer is simply relating a story objectively. But when you sense a "disconnect" between the story and the way it's being told, pay attention to the feelings being evoked, and try to identify the attitude that might be behind it. If you can describe the tone with precision, you have read insightfully and your essay will be the stronger for your deep thought.

Of course, what happens in the story matters, but in considering essay topics, look beyond the facts of the story to the art of the telling, and how it conveys the *sense* of the story. This involves addressing some of the elements that make up a work of fiction, such as the way that the setting affects the mood of the text. Consider how a gloomy atmosphere can suggest sadness, confusion, or foreboding, and look for similar kinds of setting clues in the text. Details about the characters—what they wear, how they move, what objects are associated with them—also reveal aspects of their inner lives and motivations. Your understanding of human nature can help to unpack gestures and actions, just as you would in real life. Think about how you would react in the same situation, and ask why the characters act and speak as they do.

Many adults have fond memories of English class. That is because fictional characters who act and move in fictionalized worlds can do more than entertain you, they can make you wiser. Their problems might be foreign to you, but as they suffer the consequences of their mistakes, they contribute to the growth of your judgment. So extract all the wisdom you can, by considering the moral and ethical implications of the story, by empathizing with the characters' motivations, and by probing the way that the writer's language manipulates your emotions. Delve into literary works as though your future soul depends on it, for in a way, it does.

Questions to Ask when Analyzing Fiction

Theme

- What larger idea or value lies at the heart of the work?

- What principles seem to be at stake?

Character

- If a character undergoes a transformation, what values also shifted?

- What influences contribute to a character's situation and decisions?

- Why did the character act or not act as you expected?

- What effect do minor characters and stock (stereotypical) characters have on the work as a whole?

- Is there a character who acts as a foil or opposite of the protagonist (main character) such that thinking of both of them reveals insights about the larger meaning of the text?

Plot

- Where does the action of the plot come to a point of crisis, departure, or change?

- How is the action of the plot resolved?

- How do choices in details contribute to the overall mood or sense of the text?

- What do deviations from a chronological telling contribute to the sense of the text as a whole?

- Are there instances of irony that raise expectations for one thing and produce another?

  ○ Possible types of irony: verbal (play of words), situational (unexpected consequences), cosmic (an indifferent universe rules), dramatic (a character's unique lack of knowledge leads him astray).

Setting

- How do aspects of setting reflect the situation or state of mind of the characters?

- Does the setting confirm or work against the prevailing mood of the text?

- What information about the time period does the setting contribute?

Narration

- What is the type of narrative voice?

  ○ Possible types of narrators: omniscient (all-knowing), limited (knowing only one or few characters' thoughts), unreliable (naïve or biased), characterized (playing a role in the story).

- What does the narrator seem to think about the characters, actions, and events?

- How does the narrator affect the reader's awareness of the implications of events?

- Does the narrator seem to represent the writer's views?

Language

- Is there a pattern of diction (word choice) that contributes to the overall mood or tone?

- How do modifiers such as adjectives used by the narrator indicate attitude?

- Do certain words or phrases evoke a domain of ideas (birth, death, money, solitude, etc.) that is either consistent with or in opposition to the overall message?

- What does a character's language reveal about his or her social status, education, profession, attitude, or state of mind?

- Are the characters presented in a sympathetic light, or are they held up for judgment?

- What tone conveys the author's attitude toward the events or ideas in the text?

  o Possible tone descriptors: artificial, bombastic, cautious, concerned, detached, folksy, humorous, moralistic, nostalgic, passionate, pedantic, pretentious, scholarly, skeptical, wary. Often the tone is complex and thus requires a modifier and noun, or two adjectives: restrained rage or humorous yet wary.

- How does figurative language (imagery, metaphor, simile) contribute to the overall meaning of the text?

Metaphors and analogies can "map" attributes of one object to another, such that the reader sees an idea in a new way. Here is an example:

> Slowly, over the years, Estha withdrew from the world. He grew accustomed to the uneasy octopus that lived inside him and squirted its inky tranquilizer on his past. (*The God of Small Things*, Arundhati Roy)

The metaphor of an "uneasy octopus" not only beautifully describes the physical discomfort that accompanies guilt, it also resonates to larger themes in the novel of grasping, tentacle-like relationships.

An allusion to another work, to a historical event, or person, can hint at a theme, establishing a grander purpose to the events. Clues in the pacing and cadence can attest to the narrative mood, and symbolism illuminates thematic significance. Training your eye to note literary techniques as you read enhances your ability to appreciate the writer's craft as well as the tale. In great literature, the form of the language conveys an aspect of the story.

Characterization can be established through careful choice of details. In the following passage, notice how the descriptions of two characters reveal their attitudes and faults:

> Macalister was in a purple velvet jacket over a Hawaiian shirt; his denim pants were worn out and bulging at the knees, as though he spent his days kneeling; he wore open-toe Birkenstocks with white socks; everything on him looked hand-me-down. He was in his fifties but had a head of Bakelite-black hair, so unyielding it seemed it had been mounted on his head decades before and had not changed its form since. Without expressing any identifiable emotion, he was listening to the ambassador, who was rocking back on his heels, pursing his lips, slowly passing out a thought. Macalister was drinking water; his glass slanted slightly in his hand so the water edge repeatedly touched the brim only to retreat, in the exact rhythm of the ambassador's rocking. (Aleksandar Hemon *Love and Obstacles*)

Here is a student analysis of the passage:

> Bosnian writer Aleksander Hemon paints a portrait of two pompous characters in vivid imagery, with incisive details. One portrait displays Macalister, a famous American writer, disdainfully attending a reception in his honor. The other is a U.S. ambassador. Macalister insults the occasion with his garishly mismatched, tawdry clothing but at the same time reveals his falsely inflated sense of self with a decades-out-of-style "Bakelite" hairstyle. The ambassador, self-importantly "rock[s] back on his heels" delivering a trite observation through pretentiously pursed lips. The bored Macalister entertains himself by tipping the water in his glass to the rhythm of the ambassador's rocking. Hemon's camera-like sentences pan the scene and pile on details in layers of innuendo, each phrase adding to the reader's growing amusement at two poignant examples of human egotism.

The student insightfully describes how the writer reveals the personalities of two eccentric characters through their clothing and minute gestures, and also explains the significance of these details, the basis for an excellent essay.

Analyzing Poetry

Analyzing poetry entails an intensified study of language, for poetry condenses language to compact efficiency. The poet chooses from an extensive toolbox of language devices to convey ideas and attitude, and to light up a response in readers. Each decision in the construction of a poem adds layers of meaning that must be probed and pondered, for while poetry often holds profound ideas in a beautiful still life, it seldom states those ideas outright.

The careful reader must unpack the significance of such devices as symbolism, imagery, metaphor, rhythm, cadence, and sounds. Each element potentially carries both a literal meaning and a suggested significance or nuance. For example, flower references can suggest the briefness of time, or the splendor of nature, or a reminder to pause and enjoy one's life. How do you decide which of these or other meanings it conveys? The poem has its own integrity, its own "physics," so consider how the device works within the context of the poem as a whole. A rose or a tiger or a starry sky in one poem may signify something quite different in another. Brainstorm connotations and associations and then look for a pattern. Once you arrive at a theory, test it by finding confirming evidence in other parts of the poem.

Questions to ask about poetry:

- What can be inferred about the speaker and apparent auditor of the poem?

- What do the rhyme scheme (end rhymed, enjambment, slant rhyme, etc.), rhythm (iambic pentameter, etc.), and sounds (assonance, alliteration, cacophony, etc.) contribute to the sense of the poem?

- What large ideas are engaged or in conflict?

- If there is a pattern of diction that alludes to a seemingly separate domain of thought, how does that domain help to illuminate the poem's central ideas?

- What is the tone of the poem, and what does this imply about the speaker's attitude toward the subject of the poem?

Here is an example paragraph from a student's analysis of Shakespeare's Sonnet 30 (see page 3 for the text of the poem):

> It is apparent from both the words and the sounds of this poem that the narrator's mourning is self-inflicted. His sadness comes when the memory is recalled in "sweet silent sessions," which are only "sweet" to someone who prefers to wallow in self-pity. Even the assonance ("Woe to woe" and "Bemoaned moan") and alliteration ("grieving at grievances") attest to a kind of harmony or pleasure in sadness. These and other repeated phrases and sounds make the experience seem familiar and therefore almost welcome. There are also many references to accounting: "account," "pay," "canceled," "expense." The narrator grieves at having his wasted life, at not having achieved what he "sought." But the balance sheet terminology contributes to a sense that while there are many woes on one side, there is a balancing item in the other column. The couplet raises the presence of a loved one ("dear friend") to whom the sonnet is dedicated, who exists as a single line item whose presence cancels out all of the woe, restoring the speaker's losses and returning him to a state of equanimity.

The student has addressed many poetic devices, but more importantly, has tied these aspects to an interpretation of what the poem means.

To help you think about ways to analyze fiction and poetry, here are some sample sentence stems that you might use in a literary essay:

- The tone/pace/mood shifts from x to y.

- The setting echoes (or seems to approve, or seems to disapprove) the mood of x.

- The rhythm of the line suggests (or undercuts, echoes, propels, contrasts with, etc.) x.

- The pattern of x (alliteration, rhyme, assonance, etc.) links/contrasts the ideas of y and z.

- The pace reveals a sense of x.

- The metaphors/simile/extended metaphor of x conveys that y.

- The diction lends an element of x (humor, solemnity, playfulness, irony, dignity, etc.).

- The symbolism of x suggests y.

- The *x* narrative point of view of (omniscient, effaced, characterized, editorial, naïve, unreliable, first-person, second-person, etc.) contributes a sense of *x*.

- The rhyme scheme suggests a sense of *x* (predictability, ordinariness, triteness, completeness, closure, etc.).

- The rhythm creates a mood of *x* (playfulness, motion, discord, unity, etc.)

- The writer's attitude can best be described as *x* based on *y* and …

Analyzing Non-Fiction

Essays, speeches, and many (some say all) other works of literature present an argument—they take a position on a topic and attempt to convince the reader of the truth of that position. The best arguments convince through a variety of tactics, including making strategic concessions to develop a rapport with their audience, asking challenging rhetorical questions that compel the audience to think, lining up evidence to counter assumptions, quoting authorities to capitalize on their reputation for knowledge, and playing upon cultural assumptions and values to establish connections with the audience. Arguments, whether persuasive essays, advertisements, or works of art, attempt to demonstrate consistency with the audience's core values through appeals to logic, compassion, justice, patriotism, and so on. The author also appeals to the audience by establishing a strong *ethos* or persona from which to make the argument, building credibility through appropriate diction, displaying an array of knowledge about the topic, mentioning experiences with the topic, etc.

Questions to ask about non-fiction texts:

- What kind of ethos or persona does the narrator establish?

- What appeals to the audience are made, and how do they operate?

- How does the writer establish common ground with the audience?

- What kind of reasoning is employed?

  - Deductive (reasoning from evidence), inductive (reasoning from one claim to another), cause-effect (analyzing potential or actual consequences), pro/con (analyzing relative merit), comparison/contrast (analyzing attributes), etc.

- What concessions are admitted?

- How are possible objections refuted?

- What is the tone or mood of the piece? Does it change?

- Is there significance to any unexpected juxtaposition or sudden shift in topic or pace?

In the following excerpt from William Faulkner's three-minute 1950 Nobel Banquet speech, notice how the speaker creates common ground, establishes an ethos of authority, and appeals to the audience's sense of pride and honor:

> Our tragedy today is a general and universal physical fear so long sustained by now that we can even bear it. There are no longer problems of the spirit. There is only the question: When will I be blown up? Because of this, the young man or woman writing today has forgotten the problems of the human heart in conflict with itself which alone can make good writing because only that is worth writing about, worth the agony and the sweat.

> He must learn them again. He must teach himself that the basest of all things is to be afraid; and, teaching himself that, forget it forever, leaving no room in his workshop for anything but the old verities and truths of the heart, the old universal truths lacking which any story is ephemeral and doomed – love and honor and pity and pride and compassion and sacrifice. Until he does so, he labors under a curse. He writes not of love but of lust, of defeats in which nobody loses anything of value, of victories without hope and, worst of all, without pity or compassion. His griefs grieve on no universal bones, leaving no scars. He writes not of the heart but of the glands.

The excerpt is from the middle of the speech, which he began by indicating that he was speaking generally to writers everywhere. Perhaps you can guess that Faulkner next expresses his own determination not to fall victim to triteness and to write about "the old verities" of honor and courage, and he calls upon other writers to join him in this endeavor.

Here are some sentence stems that you might use in an essay analyzing non-fiction:

- The writer creates common ground with the audience by x.

- The writer establishes authority/credibility through x

- The steps of the logic in the argument are x, y, and z.

- The writer makes the strategic concession of x which has the effect of y.

- The writer exposes/commits the logical fallacy of x by saying y, in that…

- The writer appeals to the audience's sense of x by mentioning y.

- The analogy of x aids the reader in understanding y.

- The statistic/anecdote/imagery/personal appeal/process analysis/etc. appeals to the reader's logic/compassion/ethics/sense of justice/etc.

- The humor of x has the effect of y.

- The writer evokes x in order to y.

- The writer acknowledges opposing arguments by saying x.

- In saying x, the writer implies y.

- The writer's tone conveys a sense of x (profundity, comedy, urgency, etc.).

Summing Up

When analyzing literature, you must not only understand the words on the page but the dynamics between the author and the reader to address the many ways in which a writer achieves his purpose. This means slowing down and asking *how* the text is working. Here are some aspects to consider:

The author's perspective: purpose, context, authorial persona, attitude, bias, point of view, tone

The narrative point of view: omniscient, limited, characterized, effaced, unreliable, naïve, objective; first person ("I"), second person ("You"), third person, etc.

The effect on the reader: intended audience, appeals (to emotion, authority, justice, etc.)

The rhetorical devices in the text: hyperbole, parallel structure, diction, dialect, syntax, figurative language, imagery, symbolism, repeated motifs, allusions, sensory language, satire, irony, humor, themes, etc.

The arguments that are made: logic, logical fallacies, rhetorical questions, evidence (reliability, adequacy, accuracy), inductive and deductive reasoning, concessions

The way the text is structured: organization, pace, shifts, contrasts, juxtapositions, setting, mood

See sample Poetry Analysis and Art History essays in Appendix.

2.3   For History and Other Social Science Essays

To understand is to perceive patterns. —*Isaiah Berlin*

God cannot alter the past, though historians can. —*Samuel Butler*

The study of the events and purposes of humankind is a restless, moving target. Take heart against the fear that everything has already been said about history, sociology, political science, and the other social sciences. Historical scholarship—research and analysis—is based on that which has gone before. It is extremely unlikely that someone will discover a past event or phenomenon; more likely, a scholar will rework older material (theory and evidence) into a new framework, providing a fresh perspective. The same holds true for the other social sciences: economics, journalism, sociology, political science, government, etc. The past and present are so complex that another attempt to bring clarity to a topic is welcome. Do your part to clarify things when you write, and you will write a successful essay.

As you prepare to write an essay in the social sciences, as in other disciplines, let your curiosity guide you; find a conflict, enigma, or pattern that puzzles and interests you. And then, as in other disciplines, research accompanied by sustained free-writing will lead to a viable thesis. Allow Who, What, When, Where, How, and Why questions to shape your thinking, expanding on each one as you burrow into the details to find a pattern. Start with the first four in order to fathom the more complex How and Why questions, which will be the heart of your essay. You can begin this process right away, to remind you what to research, and ask these questions again in the middle of your reading, to make sure you have covered everything you need.

For a given event or idea, ask:

- Who did what to whom? Who contributed, obstructed, fought, led, supported, or ended it? Who was affected by it?

- What preceded, contributed to, influenced or was influenced by, followed, was caused by, or happened concurrently? What values did it oppose, violate, honor, or call into question?

- When did it start, build, decline, end, restart, resurge, or alter?

- Where did it come from, proceed, end up? Where else did it occur, or might it occur?

- How did it shape, influence, or catalyze other events or ideas? How did it work? How do or did political, social, economic, technical, intellectual, or international factors influence the topic or idea?

- Why was it noticed, ignored, accepted, decried, applauded, condoned, enshrined, etc.?

Sample Who, What, When, Where, How, and Why analysis:

Topic:	The Second Punic Wars
Who:	Carthaginians (Hannibal) versus Romans (Scipio Africanus)
What:	Conflict over control of the western Mediterranean Sea, won by Rome
When:	218 to 202 BC
Where:	Primarily in modern-day Italy and Tunisia
How:	Elephant cavalry, trireme ships, foot soldiers, spears, spikes, and swords
Why:	On Hannibal's part, revenge; on Rome's part, consolidation of power on peninsula as well as on the sea
Working thesis:	The masses of both peoples suffered more than the elite Romans, who prospered because of the war

In doing research, use both primary sources (from the time period, such as letters, memoirs, speeches, and so on) and secondary sources (those that interpret or analyze, such as journal articles, monographs, and the like). A textbook can provide background information prior to deeper research. Also consider non-textual artifacts—stone markers, monuments, tools, and weapons—as these can be particularly revealing. Consider the writer's point of view and any limitations the writer might have in terms of bias or access and insight into the topic or event. Does the writer's political affiliation or social status or level of education affect the reliability of the account? Remember that "History never looks like history when you are living through it" (writer John W. Gardner) so eyewitnesses may unintentionally present a distorted view. It is equally important to consider any bias in sources. Make sure that the scope of your topic is neither too broad nor too narrow for the length of essay you will write.

As your thesis takes shape, think of your essay as a case to be presented in court: you must advocate for the perspective you consider accurate. However, make any necessary concessions rather than ignore or steamroller over the opposing viewpoint. Consider your audience to be only mildly skeptical, willing to listen to reason but unwilling to accept a one-sided account. If your research becomes overwhelming, as it can, it can help to formulate your ideas by completing the following statements:

I want to prove that _____.

To demonstrate that I have considered opposing views, I must concede that _____.

So far I have evidence that proves _____.

To complete my proof, I need evidence that says _____.

I need to define these terms _____.

I can vouch for the reliability of my primary sources because they _____.

I can account for biases or limitations of my secondary sources by _____.

A reader could challenge my thesis with _____, but I will counter this view with _____.

Of course, you will not use these phrases in your essay. Do this just to take stock of where you so that you can proceed efficiently.

In writing an essay for a social science class, you may be able to adapt the following template to create a comprehensive and clear thesis statement:

Concession	Topic	Verb	Value or Result	Reasons or Methods
although/while/ since	subject and claim	active verb	freedom/ failure	because/by

Examples:

> Although he calmed international relations for the United States, ultimately, President Obama's conciliatory policies weakened the Democratic Party by making too many concessions to the right-wing conservatives who dominated the Congress.

> Despite his charismatic command, his seasoned troops, and a brilliant military strategy, Napoleon's arrogance led inevitably to his defeat at Waterloo, for it prevented him from properly assessing the skills of his generals and factoring in the weather conditions.

As you write the essay, balance analytical writing with description and narrative along with relevant quoted evidence. Include short anecdotes that tell a story and paint a picture for the reader's mind, using sensory details. Notice how the passage below brings a scene to life while explaining how and why things occurred as they did. This sort of anecdote also makes for a wonderful introductory hook that captures the reader's attention immediately.

> In an Internet café in Cairo, a dozen unemployed young men silently hunch over a keyboard, while images flicker to life and are quickly replaced with another, and another. Miles away, in a modest Egyptian apartment, a father picks up his new iPhone and asks his eight-year-old daughter Juju, "What advice would you give to the President of Egypt today?" At the end of Juju's message, she leans forward and whispers to President Mubarak, "And by the way, some of your police officers are removing their jackets and they're joining the people." Minutes later, all of the young men in the Internet café hear her reply. Hours later, most of the world has seen the 51-second video. The power of the Internet galvanized the revolutionists. Facebook pages listed gathering sites and advised what to do if tear-gassed (gargle and rinse out nostrils and eyes). When protesters filled Tahrir Square in Cairo demanding change, they carried

signs that said "Down with Murbarak," as well as signs saying "Thank you, Facebook."

There is a certain tone and point of view to adopt in a social sciences essay: it is the perspective of the patient inquirer, one who weighs the evidence and eventually formulates a theory that is well supported by the evidence, all of which is thoroughly explained, cited, and analyzed, and the best essays pull it all together into a compelling story.

Sample sentence stems for analysis in social sciences:

- The contribution of x has been overlooked because y

- The impact of event (or movement) x reveals a shift in y

- The role of x was indispensible (or irrelevant, influential, etc.) in y

- The shift in idea x resulted from event y (causality)

- The shift in idea x corresponded with event y (coincidence)

- The confluence of factors a, b, and c result in condition d

- The primary/instigating/contributing cause of x was y

- Although study/theory x concludes y, it fails to account for z

- Theory x which explains situation a, also explains situation b

- Since situation a led to b, parallel situation x may also lead to b

- Although it has been assumed that x, findings y suggest instead that z

- The consensus has been that x, however, it is likely that y

Summing Up

History and other social science essays explain an event or idea and offer a thesis that explains How or Why occurring an event or idea. A good social science essay does not have to break new ground or invent a new theory but can succeed by explaining a topic clearly. The essay should balance the use of analysis and plenty of quoted evidence from both primary and secondary sources with short anecdotes and bold imagery that paint a picture in the reader's mind. Include information about and observations of relevant artifacts (weapons, tools, art objects) as well. The purpose is to take a strong stand and clarify the topic while making necessary concessions and accounting for limitations in the sources used.

History and other social science essays include:

- An interesting topic suitable for the scope of the essay
- A thesis statement that asserts How or Why
- An approach similar to a case in court
- Plenty of quoted material from primary and secondary sources
- Assessment of possible bias or limitations in sources
- Descriptions and possibly images of pertinent artifacts
- Anecdotes that bring events to life
- Clear explanations
- Concessions to opposing views
- Assumptions made
- Analogies and metaphors to explain concepts or complex events
- Vivid language
- Reference list of sources consulted

See sample Philosophy and Political Science essays in Appendix.

2.4   For Science Essays

> Every scientific statement must remain *tentative forever*. It may indeed be corroborated, but every corroboration is relative to other statements which, again, are tentative. —*Karl Popper*

What you learn in your science classes may be the most important material you can encounter, because you may be lucky enough to contribute to a solution to one of the many problems plaguing the world today. So, buckle down, please, and learn your science and write terrific essays for your classes so you can make the rest of us grateful! Do not succumb to the fear that you can add nothing new to the discipline. As philosopher Karl Popper explains above, scientific knowledge constantly evolves, requiring new voices to express new ideas. Even when you write about established science, your fresh and vivid explanation can spark your reader's imagination, enlivening "old" news.

American science fiction writer Isaac Asimov once said "The most exciting phrase to hear in science, the one that heralds new discoveries, is not 'Eureka!' (I found it!) but 'That's funny ...'" He is referring to the fact that once the discovery in science occurs, the best part of science is over. The fun part starts when the scientist notices an anomaly that requires further investigation. Therefore, science essays about interesting problems can be just as significant and exciting to write about as those announcing solutions. You don't have to invent a cure for cancer, discover a new genome, or end global warming to write an excellent essay in astronomy, biology, anatomy, environmental science, chemistry, physics, or botany. All you have to do is illuminate the topic and intrigue the reader as you explain how a process works or why an event did or might occur, and you will succeed. That means that in science, as in other disciplines, there is an art to writing well. Make a good analogy or explain a complex process in clear, direct language, and you will have contributed something meaningful. However, keep in mind your goal to learn as much as you can from the experience as well. What you learn about an ancient fossil or an algal bloom may contain the germ of an idea that will change the world for the better.

Many science courses do not require essays, but rather lab reports or précis (summaries) of scientific articles. For that kind of writing, your instructor will guide you. This section offers guidelines for essays that you may be required to write. There are important differences between science essays and essays on novels or poems. One big difference is that when writing about science, you usually do not quote your sources, but summarize or paraphrase them. Your goal here is to demonstrate your understanding of the points the source has made. Be careful to represent the ideas responsibly, preserving the sense of the original text. The other big difference is that longer science essays are usually organized into sections, with subtitles, and they begin with an abstract, which offers a thumbnail summary of the essay. Also, many science essays do not present a thesis. Instead, they simply present a question that the rest of the essay will answer.

In developing ideas for your topic, you can start by listing the main questions within it. For example, for an essay on the genetic modification in foods, you might ask:

Has genetic modification of food seeds been successful?

How much does genetic modification increase crop yield?

How does it affect nutrition?

What unintended side effects occur?

Are genetically modified seeds transferable to other locations?

Brainstorm several questions before deciding on the one that will guide your research. Then, as you read, you can refine your working question and begin to see the outline of the essay take shape. Starting with a list of questions will save you reading time because you can quickly decide which resources are topical.

It is standard to arrange longer science essays into sections. Here are three possible outlines:

Abstract (optional)	Abstract (optional)	Abstract (optional)
Introduction	Introduction	Introduction
Statement of Problem	Background	Materials
Review of Literature	Subtopic A	Methods
Analysis of Lab/Research Results	Subtopic B, etc.	Results/Findings
Conclusion	Conclusion	Conclusion
References	References	References

Each of these sections can be divided into subsections, and some may be combined (Introduction and Background, Materials and Methods, etc.)

Here's a sample:

Abstract

Introduction: the Scope of the Food Security Problem in Africa

Lessons Learned from the Green Revolution [background]

How Can Sub-Saharan Africa Undertake a Successful Green Revolution of its Own?

Signs of Progress

Conclusion

References

During research, take notes in your own words and include page numbers. You generally do not quote material in science essays, but paraphrase it to indicate your understanding of a concept. While reading, consider the impact of established and emergent theories, and try to determine any potential bias of sponsorship. Look at the bibliographies of the sources you are already using to find other possible sources.

Include visual representations as well. In your research you may find a chart or diagram that perfectly sums up the data you need. Copy that into your notes and embed it into your essay if needed. You can also include your own drawings and tables.

You may have your own lab results or research to include. Present this material in the same professional manner as research from established scientists, and be sure to note any possible anomalies or test conditions that might compromise your data. Unless the results are conclusive, express your findings as tentative or speculative and suggest what additional research would be needed to confirm them.

Write in a brisk, efficient, formal, but lively style. Use both inductive (inferring knowledge from data) and deductive (following a chain of logic) reasoning to explain conclusions. Use analogies or metaphors to help the reader imagine the structure of the topic. Use bold imagery and storytelling elements to enliven your writing, without allowing these elements to distort the facts. Use accurate scientific terms, and define them as necessary for your audience. Let the reader know that you have enjoyed your research and the writing of your essay.

Here are some sample sentence stems for scientific analysis:

- The confluence of factors a, b, and c result in conditions d

- Theorem x does/does not apply to situation y because of factor/anomaly z

- Factor x plays a crucial role in process y

- The data/findings from table/graph x indicate/suggest/prove/confirm that y

- We can infer from these findings that x.

- Study *x* is inconclusive because it lacks *y*

- Study *x* is convincing because it demonstrates/accounts for *y*

- Factor *x* explains *y*

- Factor *x* is made possible by *y*

- One explanation for *x* has been has been *y*; however explanation *z* might also apply

- The presence of element *x* in environment *y* has had the effect of *z*

- The essential difference between organism (or process, etc.) *x* and *y* is *z*

- The conditions of environment *x* are/were ripe for *y*

- Although it has been assumed that *x,* recent findings instead suggest/demonstrate that *y*

- Results *x* are unclear/inconclusive/speculative because *y*

As you conduct your research, whether from your own experiments and observations or through the available literature, be sure to assess the logic of the findings. Ask yourself the following questions:

Have I verified my results?

Have I stated my assumptions?

Have experiment conditions been properly controlled?

Might some other factor account for the results?

In your paper, address any unresolved factors that might have affected the outcome or conclusions. It is better to address these upfront rather than cause skepticism in the reader.

Summing Up

Science essays explain an idea, a process, a situation, or offer a hypothesis about an outcome or a reason for a situation. Therefore, the key to a good science essay is to explain yourself clearly, yet artfully, so as both to inform and to entertain. Structure longer essays into sections, and begin with an abstract that condenses the essay into a few precise sentences at the beginning. Include analogies, metaphors, charts, graphs, and diagrams to help the reader to understand complex data and concepts.

Science essays include:

- Optional sections (Abstract, Introduction, named subsections, Conclusion)
- Sources that are faithfully paraphrased, not quoted
- Figures, charts, diagrams, drawings, tables
- Clear explanations
- Inductive and deductive reasoning
- Assumptions made
- Analogies and metaphors for structural concepts
- Vivid language
- Findings that are identified as either speculative or confirmed
- Reference list of sources consulted

See sample Science Research and Environmental Science essays in Appendix.

2.5   For Essays on Visual Media

Why do people visit art museums or watch films? To attain culture, some would say, or to experience the sublime, to explore other times and cultures, or to be surprised, delighted, and moved. But often, despite standing thoughtfully in front of a work of art for an extended time, the visitor fails to read all the layers of the work, to analyze it thoroughly. Yet the visual rhetoric of any work of art operates on several levels: aesthetic, intellectual, and social. Art can reinforce beliefs, inspire values, advance social enterprises, and reinforce cultural norms, through composition as well as subject. Often, the most important messages occur below the level of conscious awareness. Just as in advertising (where, for example, a woman shown lounging in an expensive dress and jewelry implies that wearing a certain brand of perfume lends an air of wealth and social status), the composition and content of visual art convey socially important values. The arrangement of characters in a monument can suggest relative status in the social hierarchy, a misty landscape painting can romanticize expansion, and an oversized equestrian sculpture can convey majesty and power. An old-fashioned setting can contribute nostalgic value to the subject displayed in it. And the posture of the subject can convey such attitudes as pride, humility, wonder, subordination, fear, respect, etc. Be sure to consider the artist's purpose, the effect on the viewer, and composition elements in your analysis. You also need your interpretive skills to understand the more practical visual art present in charts, diagrams, and maps. The creator's biases, purpose, and cultural influences affect the overall impact of the data. Also, be sure to assess the completeness, pertinence, and sufficiency of evidence, as well as the reliability of the sources used, before accepting the conclusions drawn from them.

Analyzing Film

We watch films to be terrified, scandalized, entertained, or emotionally moved. According to French filmmaker Jean-Luc Godard, cinema is "the most beautiful fraud in the world, because its visual and sound impressions can resonate as deeply as a lived memory." Therefore, it can be difficult to maintain a critical distance instead of simply being drawn into its world. You may have to view a film more than once to detect the elements unique to the art of filmmaking that create such profound effects. The way that scenes are mixed through editing affects our understanding of the events being related. The camera angle deliberately places the viewer, and even that decision carries interpretive meaning. Soundtracks, sound effects, and special effects also play important roles in communicating ideas and values. All of these combine to draw in the viewer, whose relationship to the action is manipulated by the director's choices. Does the director invite the audience to view the film from a safe distance, or does the viewer feel involved in the action, with sweaty palms and increased heart rate? Is the action handed over as to a voyeur, creating a sense of undetected intimacy? Are you as the viewer invited into another world or does the film keep presenting reminders of its constructed nature?

Here is renowned film critic Pauline Kael commenting on a car chase scene in the 1974 film *The Sugarland Express* by director Steven Spielberg:

> Spielberg is a choreographic virtuoso with cars. He patterns them [vehicles]; he makes them dance and crash and bounce back. He handles enormous configurations of vehicles; sometimes they move so sweetly you think he must be wooing them. These sequences

are as unforced and effortless-looking as if the cars themselves—mesmerized—had just waltzed into their idiot formations... The cars have tiffs, wrangle, get confused. And so do the people, who are also erratic and—in certain lights—eerily beautiful.

Kael identifies a correspondence between car chase scenes and the erratic relationships between the characters in the films, in her own beautiful expression. Here is a student sample from an essay comparing two film versions of *Hamlet*:

> The sound tracks of both the Olivier and the Branaugh version of *Hamlet* include stringed orchestral music, but with widely differing effects. Branaugh's soundtrack has a much lighter mood, particularly when Hamlet and Ophelia confess their love for one another. During this scene, the higher stringed instruments, violins in particular, play a vibrato-heavy and lyrical phrase that acts as a light and blissful contrast to the dark tone of the rest of the film. In Olivier's film, a single bass creates a low ambient drone to signal the presence of the ghost in Gertrude's chamber; an interesting contrast to the more traditional sounds in the rest of the film. The drone sounds almost alien, and is effective at showing the supernatural character of Hamlet's vision. Music in both of these versions of *Hamlet* creates a distinct mood and underscores the emotions of their characters.

Your film essay should include the artistic elements of the film as well as the themes and characterizations. It should not simply summarize the plot, but should include enough of the plot to allow someone who has not seen the film to appreciate your insights. Just be cautious about allowing the story to overwhelm your analysis of the film as a work of art.

In analyzing films, consider such elements as: focal point, framing, setting, pace, soundtrack, perspective, lighting, staging, costumes, archetypes, mis-en-scene, camera angle and distance, mood, special effects, plot development, etc.

Analyzing Images

Every work of art makes a statement that engages prevailing ideas and proposes its own values or asks probing questions. Sometimes the statement is an argument that the artist intended, but sometimes, values that the artist shares with contemporaries gain expression without being intended. Our job as viewer is to piece together the values transmitted by the work of art, through close observation enhanced by careful research into the artist and her times. With the tools to analyze paintings, sculptures, photographs, and even advertisements, the viewer can move beyond an initial esthetic or emotional response to a greater understanding of human endeavors. With skill in "reading" a work of art along with awareness of and appreciation for the ideas and values of the time period and of the artist who created it, one can reach a deep interpretation that can make for a fascinating essay.

When analyzing an image, first spend time just taking notes on your reactions to it. Where is your eye initially drawn? What does the arrangement or posture suggest? What is placed higher in the work, and what is placed lower? Consider the positioning of faces. A character who looks directly at the viewer confronts her with forthrightness, power, or intimacy. A three-quarter view can invite your view in a way that is more voyeuristic. Read facial expressions as well as indications of status represented by clothing, surroundings, and objects. Record your impressions of the use of color, pattern, light, and so on. There is a big difference in interpretation when a subject is bathed it light or cloaked in darkness. What emotions do these elements evoke? Write observations as quickly as they come to you, and spend enough time doing so to uncover layers of meaning.

Next you may want to do some research on the artist and the time period of the piece—both of its subject and the time it was produced. This information should not dominate your own ideas, but offer support for your own interpretation. If time permits, compare the work you are analyzing to others by the artist, or of the time period.

Advertisements are a special form of art, for they have the added goal of convincing the viewer to act on the message of the ad. Ads often contain subtle messages that cue the viewer to feel desire for the product advertised, and with careful analysis, you can detect these cues and possibly learn to resist their lure. Notice how often products are presented alongside images of affluence, sexuality, and power. An advertisement for a car may include a scantily clad young woman, a cigarette ad can imply that smokers are more daring and admirable, and a watch advertisement can give the impression that this product is an indicator of affluence and power. Even the font choices contribute to the overall atmosphere.

Once you have a working thesis, try writing out your interpretation in a free-writing exercise, as a student has done (below) for this promotional photograph for the 1950s American television series *The Lone Ranger* starring Clayton Moore as the Lone Ranger and Jay Silverheels as his partner Tonto. Before you read the student's analysis, ask yourself what inferences can be made about the television series from this image.

Here is a student's analysis of the photograph:

> The Indian character is dressed in animal skin, which implies an animal nature, a closeness to the outdoors. The white actor wears a spotlessly clean white outfit (in the middle of the dusty wild west), which suggests his superiority and pureness of purpose. Their relative position conveys a marked difference in power: Jay Silverheels is crouching in a subordinate physical position to Clayton Moore, as though accepting his lesser status. The Lone Ranger, with his gun out of the holster, looks ready for anything, while Jay Silverheels appears cautious, even worried, awaiting a cue from his superior before taking action. Both are

extremely fit and ready for action. They seem very compatible, as though they can instinctively rely upon one another. It can be inferred that in the series, the Lone Ranger is fully in charge, and that Tonto's natural wisdom is often called upon in their fight for justice in the old West.

The writer has scrutinized the posture and relative positions of the characters, their clothing, and their facial expressions, and has made inferences based on prevailing social values. Drawing on personal experience of human nature, too, there are many conclusions that can be drawn from these details.

Summing Up

Write essays on works of art as you would essays on other works of imagination, such as literature. You might want to embed a copy of the image in the document, and refer to elements in the image as evidence. Organize the essay according to the ideas you found in the work. In your analysis of photographs, paintings, sculptures, political cartoons, posters, advertisements, monuments, and film, consider how elements of visual rhetoric (and sound) contribute to the meaning of the piece as a whole.

When analyzing images, consider such elements as: patterns, relationships, arrangement, focal point, background/foreground, composition, symbols, mood, colors, bias, framing, grouping, narrative, title, caption, emphasis, contrasts, posture, cultural references, facial expression, movement, medium (oil, marble, wood, acrylic, etc.), genre: (still life, portrait, pastoral, landscape, domestic scene, bust, sculptural figure, decorative art, photograph), etc.

See sample Art History essay in the Appendix.

2.6   For Exam Essays

Analyzing Exam Questions

Exams are graded on not on how much detail you can produce but on how well you understand the larger questions and themes of the course.

Start by considering the implications of the exam question. Why is this question being asked? What connections can you make to key ideas and themes of the course? How can you synthesize several topics that you learned about in the course into your answer?

Preparation for writing an exam essay begins long before exam day. Having attended lectures and taken meaningful notes, a successful student will start at least a week beforehand to anticipate several possible questions the instructor might pose on the exam. Usually, the exam will address the core principles taught, so it makes sense to turn those into possible exam questions. Then write an outline for each possible question. If you first try to create the outline without referring to your notes, you will expose which areas you need to study the most. Review the outline and notes again just before the exam to refresh your memory of the approach and examples you want to use.

On the day of the exam, read the question carefully, underlining key words and phrases. Pay special attention to the *verb* of the question, as this will direct you to the kind of answer is expected.

VERB	*WHAT IS BEING ASKED FOR*
Analyze	Show how key components add up to a greater whole
Assess	Identify advantages and disadvantages and project outcomes
Compare, contrast	Evaluate the reasons for fundamental differences and similarities
Define	Explain what the topic does and does not mean and give examples
Discuss	Identify and describe the significance of key issues and give examples
Explain/Describe	Bring order to the topic by sequencing, prioritizing, or categorizing
Evaluate	Compare relative merits of pro and con positions
Illustrate	Offer typical, compelling examples that demonstrate core principles

Sample exam prompts:

- Analyze the causes and responses to the 1968 crisis in France.

- Assess the impact of the Protestant Revolution on the social order of sixteenth-century England.

- Compare the merits of non-fossil fuel options.

- Illustrate the changes in social and economic patterns that occurred along the Silk Road between 200 BCE and 1450 BCE.

- Describe the significance of the automobile in *The Great Gatsby*.

- Define force as a property of physics.

- Evaluate the pros and cons of criminalizing cyberbullying.

- For a major novel or play, discuss how a character's real or apparent madness contributes to the meaning of the work as whole.

Notice that in each of these examples, the prompt either asks for a broad understanding (the causes and consequences of…, the impact of…) or how a smaller detail (literary symbol, a character's madness) fits in to the larger picture. If you spend your time memorizing facts, you might have trouble with these exam questions. However, if you study the big picture ideas with a few examples, you can easily answer questions such as these.

When writing answers to exam questions, consider: the intention of the question, what it is asking you to do, what relationship the question has to the purposes and focus of the course. Flesh out your answer with detailed examples and link them to the ideas and broad themes of the class.

3

PREPARING TO WRITE

3.1 Free-Writing

Connecting the Dots: Free-Writing

You have already read the text with pen or stylus in hand, marking the most interesting bits (see Chapter 1). Now go back and re-read, making further observations and noticing patterns. If two or three observations seem connected, here is a good topic to explore, which you can do through free-writing. Although you might as productively just think about the topic, writing your ideas is far superior. Why? Because even your best insights can evaporate when a new idea shifts into view. Therefore, always write down your ideas, so that you can recall them later.

Start anywhere within your topic and for each annotated item or item in your notes, brainstorm ideas. Tackle the difficult-seeming passages and unlock their secrets. Explore connotations (associations between key ideas and words or phrases) and the deeper implications of the ideas you uncovered when you annotated the text. Pose questions and answer them. Probe further than your initial reactions, by asking one follow-up question, offering a tentative reply, then asking another, and another, and so on. Follow a line of thinking as far as it takes you, and even when it seems that you have exhausted this thread, keep writing. It is often at this point that your best ideas emerge.

It is fine, even commendable, to contradict yourself. No lesser superstar of writing than Walt Whitman approved of doing so in his poem "Song of Myself," when he declared, "Do I contradict myself? / Very well then....I contradict myself. / I am large….I contain multitudes." So follow up one line of reasoning with a completely antithetical line of thought.

Consider how thematic elements relate to philosophical, political, economic, social, or ideological ideas. The more thoughts you get down on paper, the more material you will have to choose from in your essay. Consider the context and implications of the problem—anticipate what might happen and consider why certain other outcomes did not occur. Literally write out these questions and try to answer them. Free-associate connections to class themes, the big ideas described by the instructor and others, and major theories associated with the discipline. For example, how does a given war fit the requirements of Just War Theory? Does the possible extinction of a given species suggest that like species might also follow suit?

What you write just after you thought you had finished will probably be your best thoughts. Cognitive scientists suggest that it takes most people twenty minutes of concentrated thinking to reach a breakthrough. Be sure to allow enough time for this to happen. At first you may find your mind wandering listlessly, but your brain will eventually engage with the ideas to produce some surprising new threads of thought. Give it time to do what it does best—making connections and finding meaning in patterns. When you read over what you have written, you will be happy that you spent this time exploring through writing.

Summing Up

To discover interesting ideas for your essay, review your annotations and comments, probe difficult passages, and free-write to discover what you think. Analysis consists of taking apart what you see in the subject and reconstructing it according to the meaning you discover.

Analysis and free-writing include:

- Unpacking complex passages

- Asking and speculating answers to questions

- Following one idea, then its antithesis

- Exploring ideas or images held in opposition

- Explaining patterns of diction, cadence, or imagery

- Exploring personal reactions

- Considering context, narrator's point of view, mood, tone, shifts

- Noticing what is significantly left out or missing

Example of free-writing on Shakespeare's Sonnet 30:

The lines keep repeating the same idea, that the narrator misses someone who is dead. The repetition draws the reader into the narrator's state of mind, sensing the immediacy of the pain of mourning, a burden that keeps reappearing. Even in the poem; the memory won't go away. But it is a memory from the past. The narrator has recalled it, called it into his mind. This happens often, apparently, because the first two lines indicate a pattern of behavior: "When...I..." When he succumbs to these memories, or sweet sessions, this memory comes back. No, he summons it. He purposely calls it back. The narrator wants to see the loved one again. There are lots of references to sight—"a vanished sight," "eye," "precious friends hid." Is the narrator mourning one or many missed loved ones? The eye cannot see because it is drowned in tears. So is the eye seeing correctly? It seems like a vision that haunts through absence. Is this mourning self-inflicted? It is, because the sadness comes when the memory is recalled in "sweet silent sessions." "Sweet"? That's strange. Yes, it is sort of "sweet" to wallow in misery, self-pity. Even the assonance and alliteration attest to a kind of harmony or pleasure in "grieving at grievances." Shakespeare of all poets could have come up with another word to avoid repeating himself. Grieving grievances. Woe to woe. Bemoaned moan. The repeating pattern makes it seem predictable, familiar. The narrator also senses having wasted life, and not having gotten what he "sought." There are a lot of references to accounting: account, pay, canceled, expense. It's like a summing up, or an accounting sheet with woes on one side, and the one who restores losses on the other. Woes versus one. Tightly linked by sound. Lots of oh, oh, oh sounds in lines 9-12. Sadness, or rapture? The "solution" doesn't occur until the end. And there is no longing for that one. That idea comes unbidden, suddenly, separated from the rest of the poem in its final couplet. Whereas the narrator "summons up" the "remembrance of things past," the relief only occurs "if." There is some contingency here that is not present in the "sweet sessions" which seemingly will always occur. Do the "Sorrows end"? Only for the moment, then the cycle will repeat.

Another example of free-writing:

> Charlotte Perkins Gilman suffered depression because she feared she
> was not a "real" woman. She had turned her back on motherhood
> and marriage. There were no precursors and no available means for
> dealing with the demands of motherhood for career women. It wasn't
> as though she could hire a nanny or babysitter. Her husband didn't
> understand. She had to make a choice, alone, against what everyone
> else wanted from her. It was a choice that women no longer have
> to make. So she was out of step with her time. She represented a
> new kind of woman, one who could pursue a career. But being
> alone in her choice, she suffered doubts and fears—was she acting
> out of selfishness? Was her message worth her sacrifices? She knew
> she had a message to deliver to the world, but the very content of
> her message was part of the reason she couldn't deliver easily. She
> martyred her own life so that she could spare the same heartaches
> for others. She envisioned a gender-fair society, a kind of utopia of
> gender rules, where females were no longer bound by definitions of
> the feminine. Her attempt to inhabit that envisioned utopia, which
> would not evolve in real life for decades, nearly undid her.

When you have discovered some interesting new ideas through free-
writing, it pays to go back and re-read the text once again, finding other
instances that support your theory or that offer meaningful contradictions
that require you to revise it. Once you have thoroughly dissected
the parts of the piece, your analysis will put them together in a new
pattern, this time in the order of the insights you have derived. Think
of analysis as taking apart a text, sorting ideas into groups or clusters, and
reconstructing a new, interpretive whole. Just make sure that your ideas
are adequately supported by the text.

3.2   Organizing

The approach described in this section starts with details—evidence—
and works its way up to deriving a thesis to contain them. There are
other ways to organize to write, such as concept mapping and outlining.
These methods help you put ideas into categories and then into order.
However, the approach outlined here allows the thesis and organization

to evolve from processing the details. Some writers (a small percentage, actually) prefer to derive a thesis first, and then find the evidence to support it. This can result in looking for the proverbial "needle in a haystack" so it is not recommended. Nevertheless, while the "details up" method works well, there are those who feel uncomfortable without having a defined thesis in hand, and who want to approach the task from the top down. If this sounds like you, start with Section 3.3. Deriving a Thesis, and then return to this section.

Also note: some assignments expect the essay not to present its thesis at the beginning, but to arrive at it through thoughtful articulation of the issues. Be sure you are clear before writing whether your essay should start—or end—with a thesis.

There are many ways to sort your evidence and examples, from putting material into separate computer documents (or index cards) to numbering each selection in the order you plan to use it, to writing the easy parts first and building the essay from the middle out. Some computer programs (such as www.evernote.com) allow you to sort note cards on the screen, trying out different sequences until you find one that you like. Before you start sequencing, use the following method to select passages in cases where the thesis is not evident and the amount of information is getting overwhelming. This method helps you make connections between related subtopics, cull out excess citations, and discover how to organize the material.

A. Selecting Passages

You have already identified possible evidence. Now you'll need to cut and paste (or write) them into a new document and assign each one a pithy phrase that succinctly identifies it. List these identifying phrases in one place, in no particular order. If the evidence items are short enough, you can simply put them into one long document (real or virtual). Don't worry yet about sequencing. Just get them into one place so you can look them over.

Example: Charlotte Perkins Gilman (American proto-feminist 1860–1935)

Hated corsets
Started exercise club for women
Fiancé thought marriage would cure her independent streak
Cried and shook when dressing her child

Husband committed her to Dr. Mitchell for the "rest cure" for "neurasthenia

Battled depression most of her life

Envisioned child care ("baby gardens") and take-out food

Proclaimed unfairness of limiting women to domestic sphere

Exposed how language conveys sexual bias against women

Said the "Ideal Woman" "has the virtues of a subject class: obedience, patience, endurance, contentment, humility"

Gave up marriage and child to pursue career of lecturing and writing

B. Grouping Passages

Now group them into categories, looking for patterns of evidence that are part of a larger idea. Two or three items might naturally go together to comprise a category of their own. For example, from the list above, a writer might group together Gilman's exercise club, her "baby garden" idea, and giving up her marriage, as all of these have to do with her innovation. Assign each group a letter or code (★, @, etc.), (codes work better than numbers, because they do not imply a sequence). At this point, you don't necessarily know which will be main ideas, which will be subordinated to other ideas, and which will be side or irrelevant issues. You won't use every idea listed, but don't eliminate anything yet unless it doesn't fit at all. Items that fit in more than one category can be double coded. You can decide later where they fit best. Finally, make a scratch outline of your categories and decide what order makes the most sense. When you begin to write, you can just follow this outline, choosing the evidence from your coded list as you go.

Example: Charlotte Perkins Gilman

Categories

I = **Innovations** she created to cope and to transform women's lives

L = how feminist issues played out in her own **Life**

T = proto-feminist **Theories** that she expounded

     L   Hated corsets

     T   Said the "Ideal Woman" "has the virtues of a subject class: obedience, patience, endurance, contentment, humility"

I Started exercise club for women

T Proclaimed unfairness of limiting women to domestic sphere

L Fiancé thought marriage would cure her independent streak

L Cried and shook when dressing her child

L Husband committed her to Dr. Mitchell for the "rest cure" for "neurasthenia

L Battled depression most of her life

I Envisioned child care ("baby gardens") and take-out food

T Exposed how language conveys sexual bias against women

I Gave up marriage and child to pursue career of lecturing and writing

Scratch outline for Charlotte Perkins Gilman:

A. **L** How feminist issues played out in her own life

 a. Hated corsets

 b. Battled depression

 c. Fiancé thought marriage would cure her independent streak

 d. Cried and shook when dressing her child

B. **I** Innovations she created to cope and to transform women's lives

 a. Started exercise club for women

 b. Envisioned child care ("baby gardens") and take-out food

 c. Gave up marriage and child to pursue career of lecturing and writing

C. **T** Proto-feminist theories that she expounded

 a. Exposed how language conveys sexual bias against women

 b. Proclaimed unfairness of limiting women to domestic sphere

 c. Said the "Ideal Woman" "has the virtues of a subject class: obedience, patience, endurance, contentment, humility"

Here's a different way to organize the same material:

1. **B (Body)** Her feminist concerns for the female body

   a. Hated corsets
   b. Started exercise club for women
   c. ?? (more research needed)

2. **M (Marriage)** Her feminist concerns in the realm of marriage

   a. Battled depression
   b. Fiancé thought marriage would cure her independent streak
   c. Said the "Ideal Woman" "has the virtues of a subject class: obedience, patience, endurance, contentment, humility"
   d. Gave up marriage and child to pursue career of lecturing and writing

3. **F (Family)** Her feminist concerns and solutions for family and community

   a. Cried and shook when dressing her child
   b. Envisioned child care ("baby gardens") and take-out food
   c. Proclaimed unfairness of limiting women to domestic sphere
   d. Exposed how language conveys sexual bias against women

Organizing the evidence codes into an outline confirmed that there is plenty of information for each category in the first version, but that additional research would be needed for the alternative outline. How much more efficient and less discouraging it is to discover this sort of problem before starting to write!

Sometimes the nature of the topic offers its own categories. For example, when writing an essay about how to feed the poor in the continent of Africa, before doing any research one can anticipate that the essay will include sections on the scope of the hunger problem, methods of increasing crop production that have worked (and not worked) in other places, successful programs within Africa, and what needs to be accomplished. After a bit of initial research reading, here is a draft outline:

Green Revolution in Africa OUTLINE

1. Problem – Scope

2. Myths and Realities of Green Rev
    a. Fertilizer
    b. Crop yields
    c. GMO
    d. Aid

3. What is Needed
    a. Micronutrients
    b. Infrastructure
    c. Irrigation
    d. Double cropping

4. Threats to Success
    a. Ethical issues (land grab, corruption)
    b. Water distribution and desertification

5. Key Players
    a. International investors/donors/aid
    b. Govt

6. Signs of Hope
    a. Conference
    b. Japan aid
    c. UN?
    d. Science/research

And here is the outline after additional reading and with some of the research notes plugged in. Notice that the writer carefully includes a citation after each paragraph so as not to get confused about where she got the text.

Green Rev in Africa OUTLINE

1. Problem – Scope

"So how much more food and land will we need in 2050? The FAO says that overall food production will need to increase by 70 per cent; annual cereal production will need to rise to about three billion tonnes from 2.1 billion tonnes today; and annual meat production will need to increase by more than 200 million tonnes to 470 million tonnes." (Rowe)

"Access to water is cited, along with energy and food security, as a key component of the "perfect storm" of resource shortages outlined by Professor John Beddington, the UK government's chief scientist; and geopolitical analysts increasingly argue that the major wars of this century are likely to be fought over water rather than land or fossil fuels." (Rowe Watershed)

"One third of Africa's population of close to a billion people is malnourished--that means over 300m people do not have enough to eat on a day-to-day basis. Africa as a whole imports more food than it produces. Yet 60% of Africa's population is directly engaged in agriculture. As Michael Foster, director of the Sasakawa-Global (SG 2000) programme in Uganda puts it: 'You cannot be on a farm and importing food!' " (Versi)

"Also, infrastructural problems have continued to serve as a barrier to Green Revolution success in Africa. Inadequate property rights protection have had the effect of blunting farmers' production opportunities and incentives, leaving little possibility for private gain in adopting new technologies. Local banks have been unable or unwilling to assist in providing the necessary loans for farmers to purchase new technologies." (Wu and Butz 24)

"The cost of fertilisers, sometimes five or six times the world average, meant exhausted land could not be replenished." (Versi Green Rev)

"The new HYV crops that were developed elsewhere in the world were not suited to African planting conditions, where the topsoil is thinner and weather patterns, such as periods of drought, are more unpredictable." (Pinstrup-Andersen and Schioler, 2001, p. 23)

"Moreover, waterways and soils have become contaminated by the large amounts of pesticides and fertilizers used on Green Revolution farmlands. Pesticides and nitrates in drinking water have proven to be detrimental to human and animal health. An unfortunate consequence of overuse of pesticides in particular areas is that crop pests have developed resistance to the pesticidal chemicals, rendering the chemicals ineffective. Indeed, these environmental spillovers have had a depressing effect on agricultural production, the very thing they were intended to improve." (Ruttan, 1998), (Wu and Butz 35)

2. Myths and Realities of Green Rev

    a. fertilizer
    b. crop yields
    c. GMO
    d. Aid

3. What is Needed

    a. Micronutrients
    b. Self-reliance
    c. Infrastructure

       "There are countries where water is very scarce, but in the majority of places, the lack of clean drinking water and sanitation is related to governance and finance," he continues. "Infrastructure hasn;t been managed, there is no support, there's improper funding, so the system doesn't work." (Rowe Watershed)

    d. Food security (land)
    e. Irrigation
    f. Double cropping
    g. Diversity of crops

4. Threats to Success

    a. Ethical issues (land grab, corruption)
    b. Water distribution and desertification
    c. Prices don't reflect externalities

5. Key Players

    a. International investors/donors/aid
    b. Govt

6. Signs of Hope

    a. Conference
    b. Japan aid
    c. UN?
    d. Science/research

Summing Up

Organizing a mass of evidence can be overwhelming if you don't have a system. Try producing a draft outline after only a little bit of general reading. Once you have read more and have a fairly comprehensive set of notes, use the method described in this chapter: put all of your evidence in front of you so that you can encode categories, play with different sequencing, and determine which areas need additional research. Then it is relatively easy to decide on a final outline.

- Select evidence passages that contain a succinct, significant, pertinent idea

- Include all ideas and evidence for now

- List your evidence in no particular order

- Use a coding system (no numbers) to try different ways to grouping or clustering ideas

- Consider common organizing principles such as:

  ○ Problem-Alternative Solutions

  ○ Cause(s)-Effect(s)

  ○ Outcome-Cause(s)

  ○ Pro-Con

  ○ Conditions-Possible Consequences

  ○ Past-Present-Future

  ○ Categories (organize by type)

These can be used in combination, too.

See the sample Political Science essay in the Appendix on food security in Africa.

3.3   Deriving a Thesis

A thesis is a sentence that is arguable and yet supportable by evidence. It is more specific and narrow than a topic area. It is not a statement of fact, for that can be verified with simple data and therefore does not require an essay to prove it. It is the sentence that governs all of your thoughts on the topic, so it serves as a one-sentence summary of the essay. A thesis statement also circumscribes the scope of the essay—letting the reader know what the essay will include and heralding the direction it will take. The thesis often comes at the end of the introduction, but might also appear at the end of the essay, and possibly even within the body of the essay, preceded by the rationale for it and followed by an analysis of the consequences of the thesis. For example, an essay on how to solve the environmental crisis might start not with a thesis statement but with several proposed approaches, assessing each within the body of the essay, and later in the essay put forth a thesis statement that suggests what research would be needed to make the best choice. It would not make sense to present such a thesis at the beginning, for the reader would not feel inclined to read the rest of the essay.

Here are three possible thesis statements for an essay on Mark Twain's *Pudd'nhead Wilson*. Which of them establishes a specific, arguable, and significant claim?

1. Mark Twain's *Pudd'nhead Wilson* is a social commentary on life in a small town during the time of slavery.

2. Mark Twain's *Pudd'nhead Wilson* tells a story of a black slave named Tom who was given the opportunity to be free, and shows how his life progresses while growing up in a society dominated by white influence.

3. In *Pudd'nhead Wilson*, Mark Twain illustrates that identity is mostly a matter of social construction, created through societal pressures, and only minimally a reflection of congenital nature.

The first example is too general and not controversial at all. The second is more detailed, but it merely states the facts of the novella; again, it is not an arguable thesis. The third example is a good thesis statement, one that can be argued as either true or false.

Here are three possible thesis statements for an essay on Food Security in Africa. Which of them establishes a specific, arguable, and significant claim?

1. The level of hunger in Sub-Saharan Africa is pervasive and African governments must develop programs to ensure that all of its people receive adequate nutrition.

2. The Green Revolution cannot work in Sub-Saharan Africa because the soil and weather conditions are different from those in India, China, Mexico and other regions where it had some success.

3. Sub-Saharan African nations can benefit from lessons learned in the first Green Revolution to institute an improved and tailored Green Revolution of their own.

The first merely states the problem, without indicating that a specific solution might exist. The second considers, but dismisses a solution without offering one in its place. The third refines a previous solution and promises that the essay will explain what precise changes will be needed, and thus is both arguable and clearly significant.

How to Derive a Thesis Statement from Evidence

Derive your thesis by boiling down the topic into one full sentence that takes into account any major objections and answers a "Why" question. Without stating it outright, allow your personal attitude to show through (Do you accept the idea? Find it praiseworthy? Worrisome? Dangerous?). If the "Why" is not at first clear, start with "What" and "How" questions. Test your thesis by identifying at least three supporting pieces of evidence. Also look for counterevidence that would disprove your thesis. Consider the opposing side. If there is no way to construct a counterargument at all, your thesis is not a debatable one, and you'll need to start over. If things still look positive, find examples from extreme cases as well as typical cases. How far does the thesis carry you? If concessions need to be made, such that the thesis holds true only under certain conditions, this qualification might need to appear in the thesis statement itself. Make sure that the scope of material needed to support the thesis can fit in the essay you are about to write. Narrow or widen it as needed. Ask yourself if it answers the "So what?" question, to make sure your topic is worthy of an essay. Finally, read over your thesis statement again, clarify your terms, and tighten up the language to make it clear, concise, and meaningful.

Here are a few templates for thesis statements, but don't be limited by them.

- [Author's] use of x and y in [title] demonstrate the belief that z.

- [Outcome] a was caused by x, y, and z.

- X will occurs whenever y.

- X will occurs because y.

- Although it seems on the surface that x, a deeper analysis shows that y.

- Although x is true, it is also true that y.

Deriving a Thesis for an Exam Question

In answering an exam question, there are many ways to begin, but do not be tempted to start writing until you have identified what the question expects you to do. Don't let the clock hurry you past the planning phase or you might answer the wrong question. No amount of eloquence can make up for irrelevance. The thesis for an exam essay consists of a focused sentence that answers the question directly and makes any necessary concessions. Often, you can just turn the question into a declarative statement. For example:

Question: How did Darwin's theories challenge existing assumptions about religion and morality?

Answer: Darwin's theories challenged existing assumptions about religion and morality by…

Other times, you will have to qualify the answer, acknowledging the factors that prevent a straightforward yes or no. For example:

Question: Is the United Nations justified in intervening in member states on behalf of oppressed minorities?

Answer: Although the United Nations is committed to respecting national sovereignty, it must intervene when minority groups are deprived of basic human rights by a corrupt or failing government.

Even if you sense that your fellow classmates are already writing furiously, take a further moment to consider what kinds of proof you will need. Draft a quick list of possible subtopics or examples in the margin, choose the best of these, and put the weakest ones in the middle. Those students writing madly around you might have started with the first idea that came to mind. If you allow yourself time to sort through several possible ideas, you will write a stronger essay.

Which of the following exam thesis statements promise to fulfill the expectations of the question?

Exam question: Was Napoleon's defeat at Waterloo inevitable?

1. Napoleon was defeated at Waterloo because his generals were ill prepared and because weather conditions made troop movement difficult.

2. Napoleon's defeat at Waterloo surprised both him and the Duke of Wellington because Napoleon had the stronger army and a strategic advantage.

3. Despite his charismatic command, his seasoned troops, and a brilliant military strategy, Napoleon's arrogance led inevitably to his defeat at Waterloo, for it prevented him from properly assessing the skills of his generals and factoring in the weather conditions.

Thesis statements 1 and 2 are certainly relevant to the question, but unfortunately they miss the main point of the question, which is about the inevitability of the outcome. Only #3 addresses this aspect, and it also supplies a reason for the inevitability—that Napoleon was blinded by arrogance.

For the Charlotte Perkins Gilman essay, a thesis might contain a combination of respect for her personal strength along with regret for the sacrifices she had to make to get her ideas out to other women and to the world. Here is one way to derive such a thesis:

What: Charlotte Perkins Gilman suffered depression and gave up her daughter to pursue a career in lecturing and writing about what was wrong with women's place in society.

How: She gave up the role of the "Ideal Woman," a role she couldn't fulfill and one she felt others should not try to fulfill.

Why: Charlotte Perkins Gilman was a visionary hero of feminist history because she persisted in living freely though it cost her dearly to step out of the traditional role of the Ideal Woman.

Notice how the how question has to be figured out, or derived. In science topics, this is the equivalent of a hypothesis that will have to be proven or disproven. Notice also how the answer to Why resulted in a thesis statement that takes a stand, indicates the writer's attitude toward the subject, and is specific, yet significant.

In the following example, the original hypothesis was "Ammonite sutures benefit the animal by making the shell stronger, and thus are evidence of evolution." Research proved this hypothesis incorrect.

What: Ammonite fossils show development of more complex sutures over time.

How: The sutures seem to be an improvement in that they are more complex, but research shows that they do not provide benefits for the animal.

Why: The development of more complex sutures in ammonites is simply an instance of random change and not evidence of evolutionary development.

Other examples:

What: In Shakespeare's *Othello*, Iago manipulates other characters.

How: He insinuates himself into their trust, exploiting their trust in order to destroy it.

Why: Initially, Iago does this in reaction to being slighted (he was not promoted), and wanting to hurt back the ones who hurt him (Othello), but later, he gets addicted to the power of controlling others' emotions.

What: In advertisements, women are put into subordinate, compromised, exposed positions.

How: The viewer sees this as evidence of a norm of sexual politics.

Why: The viewer is attracted to the sense of power in looking at someone who has less power, and thus pays attention to the advertisement. Women's images are exploited to sell products.

Sometimes you can skip the What and How steps and jump straight to a thesis, but often by slowing down in this way your thesis takes on more heft and insight, because you have moved beyond the initial analysis to something deeper.

Sample thesis statements:

Ammonite suture development demonstrates that progressive change in an attribute of a species, even when it benefits the species, is not necessarily the result of natural selection.

In Shakespeare's *Othello,* Iago loses control over his goal of revenge when he becomes addicted to the power of exploiting people's emotions.

Advertisers exploit the innate human desire for dominance by associating their product with a moment of perceived dominance over a submissive female character.

Although the United Nations is committed to respecting national sovereignty, it must intervene when minority groups are deprived of basic human rights by a corrupt or failing government.

In the Gettysburg Address, Lincoln's purpose moves from a dedication to the fallen to a summons to the survivors to make their lives worthy of the sacrificed lives being honored.

Summing Up

The thesis statement is the heart of the essay, so dedicate the time necessary to construct an excellent one. Do not settle for the obvious, overly broad, or simplistic thesis, but push for clarity and focus. Do consider whether you need to qualify the statement with necessary concessions. It must be arguable, so that your proof is worthy of attention, and specific enough to avoid large generalities, but broad enough to interest an audience. One way to make sure that you are deriving a thesis and not just a topic is to ask What, How, and then Why. Push your thinking on each of these so that you end with a genuinely interesting and debatable statement.

An excellent thesis statement:

- Governs the ideas in the essay

- Is debatable and significant

- Is neither too narrow nor too broad

- Can be thoroughly supported with reliable evidence

- Makes necessary concessions

- Addresses core ideas from the course

- Conveys your attitude toward the subject

STRUCTURING THE ESSAY

Your teacher has assigned an essay—presenting an opportunity to express your thoughts in an organized and artful manner, after careful reflection and planning. But what format will the essay take? This depends on the question or task being asked of you. Here are some things to consider before you decide on the type of essay to write. Remember that most essays are not uniquely one type—they contain elements of other essay types as well, but the overall structure can be classified as one of the following:

With few other guidelines and with no assigned source to analyze, you are probably writing a **persuasive** essay (see page 58).

If you must conduct research first, you are writing a **research** essay (see page 89).

If you have a text to analyze, no matter whether it is poetry, drama, fiction, or non-fiction, write an **explication** essay (see page 73). However, if you are asked to summarize a text, you are being asked to produce a **précis** or **summary** essay (see page 83).

If you have been asked to explain the reasons or consequences of an event, you are probably writing primarily a **cause-effect** or **problem-solution** essay (see page 68). This is an essay type that often contains elements of other essay types, such as description, comparison-contrast, classification, and definition.

If the task is to reflect upon or to consider the relative merits of an idea or thing, you are writing a **reflective** essay (see page 76) or **comparison-contrast** (or **pro-con**) essay (see page 64). But if you are asked to differentiate between members of a group, write a **classification** essay (see page 81). Alternatively, if the task requires you to explain what something means, a **definition** essay (see page 62) is called for, at least in part. Again, these elements can be combined.

If the task requires you to describe a person, place, thing, or process, write a **descriptive** essay (see page 78).

Finally, if you are preparing to write an essay for as an **exam**, see the section on Analyzing Exam Questions (page 86).

Again, most essays include aspects of several different essay formats: a persuasive essay might contain descriptive passages and a cause-effect essay might include a section of comparison-contrast writing. What follows are general guidelines that can be merged together as needed.

4.1   Types of Essay

Persuasive

The purpose of a persuasive essay is quite simple: to convince the reader that your claim is true. It is safe to assume your reader is an intelligent, reasonable person, but you cannot assume that he or she will agree with you without proof. So the writing goal is to produce an essay in which you come across as a serious, informed person making a well reasoned assertion backed up by pertinent, convincing evidence from credible sources. Your argument is your thesis, and your body paragraphs contain your proof.

In a persuasive essay, the introduction can be fairly lean, with an efficient description of the problem, the reason for its importance, and the point you are trying to make, expressed as the thesis.

Somewhere fairly early in the essay (often, right in the introduction), you should present the counterargument, the argument that opponents to your idea will hold. By attending to this right away, you build a bridge of understanding to readers. Present the argument fairly, in its strongest form. To present it at its weakest is to commit the logical fallacy (a mistake in logic that misrepresents an idea) of the "straw man" argument; i.e., an argument that is too easily dismissed. An alert reader will be put off by a self-serving dismissal of the opposing side, whether she agrees with you or not. It can only strengthen your position to begin with an appraisal of the opposition, as it puts you in the mindset of an opponent, from which vantage point you then can work your way to your own belief.

Of course, you will also want to refute the counterargument by presenting your main objections to it. Point out anomalies that the counterargument fails to handle. For example, some people feel strongly that criminals must be put behind bars to punish the guilty and to deter future crime. It takes criminals off the streets, making neighborhoods safer. However, a large percentage of incarcerated prisoners commit new crimes as soon as they are released. They return to a life of crime, often because their criminal record makes it impossible to find a real job. And in jail, they make new criminal contacts. The unintended consequence of jail time is that it stigmatizes people and reinforces habits that exclude them from living an honest life.

Now you are ready to present your claim, here, that prisons contribute to crime. Keeping the skeptical reader in mind, construct your argument using claims, evidence, and logic. Use inductive logic to extrapolate conclusions from empirical evidence, such as studies on your topic. For example, if a study shows that 70% of first-time criminals who go to jail commit new crimes upon release, you can claim that incarceration does not cure a criminal of committing crimes. Use deductive logic to build a chain of logic starting with an accepted claim or assumption that leads to a new claim. For example, you can begin with the premise that prisoners resent being isolated from society, deduce that this further alienates them from their community, and that this alienation makes it easier to commit crimes, since they do not feel attached to those they hurt. In deductive reasoning, you start with a claim that most people can accept and deduce a new claim that builds upon it, and so on, until you reach your conclusion. Your reader will be even more convinced if your claims are stated in a non-confrontational way and each is backed up with plausible, unbiased evidence and corroborating statements from reliable sources. You can also use inductive reasoning. Here, you present data and extrapolate conclusions from it. You might find a study that lists the types of crimes for which inmates are initially jailed, alongside the types of crime they commit upon release. Are these secondary crimes more, or less, serious? Be careful not to overstate the case. If a statement needs to be qualified, qualify it. You lose credibility when you make claims that the average reader knows, or can deduce, are not universally true. Also avoid the common error of circular logic, in which each claim is simply a restatement of the original claim. Your argument has to go somewhere, taking each claim to a new level of analysis.

In the body paragraphs, use ample evidence, chosen wisely. Be careful not to misrepresent the author's words. Quote the pertinent part, in as concise a manner as possible, and avoid biased sources. Where needed, define your terms, using clear, concrete terms.

Also be mindful of the way in which you present yourself. Your tone and choice of words establish an **ethos**, the persona behind they essay. You want to appear credible, informed, serious, and reliable—not high-handed, pedantic, or intolerant. Avoid grandstanding, hostile language, and anger. You want to be seen as a reasonable person making a reasonable claim.

Here are some logical fallacies to avoid:

- *Ad hominem* attack: attacking the speaker instead of the issue

- Card stacking: piling up positive evidence while ignoring opposing data

- Circular reasoning: simply restating the claim in different words

- Either/Or fallacy: assuming only two outcomes are possible

- Expedience fallacy: prioritizing goals over moral means of achieving them

- Genetic fallacy: transferring guilt due to proximity, not complicity

- Hasty generalizations: making too much of scant evidence

- Misuse of authority: citing an authority improperly

- Conclusion fallacy (*Non sequitur*): the conclusion does not follow from the premise

- Causation fallacy (*Post hoc, ergo propter hoc*): assuming that preceding events cause the events that follow

- Straw man fallacy: distorting an argument to make it easier to refute

Sample Persuasive Essay:

> The criminal justice system aims to accomplish three things: to punish and reform criminals by taking away the freedoms and privileges of citizenship, to make the streets safer by incarcerating criminals, and to deter future crime by demonstrating the cost of criminal behavior. However, the imprisonment of criminals does

not succeed in meeting the goals hoped for by society. Our prisons burgeon with inmates and costs are skyrocketing, but too often imprisoned criminals come back to society more likely than before to commit further crimes.

Punishment is designed to alter behavior, but imprisoning criminals fails to do so. Psychologists have shown that only if punishment is immediate, intense, and predictable will it convince a criminal to alter his behavior (Schwartz & Robbins, 1995). However, the criminal justice system is so clogged with cases that 85% of criminals are released before their trials (Schmalleger 35). It can then take six months, on average, to bring a criminal to trial, and, once arraigned, nine out of ten criminals avoid jail time through plea bargaining (Gest). The punishment is not swift, nor is it intense. For those who do end up in prison, the experience fails to redirect them from a life of crime. Reform efforts usually fail, possibly because of the psychological makeup of many criminals who "may be resistant to punishment even under circumstances where optimal punishment conditions apply" (Gendreau et al). And the prisons themselves become a kind of "school of crime," where offenders establish relationships with other criminals and learn of new criminal opportunities. Therefore, it will come as no surprise that a large percentage of offenders become repeat offenders. The U.S. Bureau of Justice Statistics reports that in 1994, within three years of release, over two-thirds of prisoners were re-arrested. Offenders also realize that criminal behavior is a risk worth taking, since 99.9% of crimes go undetected (Gest). With all of these outcomes in mind, it is time to take a fresh look at the goals of the criminal justice system and try to design a system that has a better chance of meting out justice, making citizens safer, and deterring crime.

Works Cited

Gest, Ted. "The Real Problems in American Justice." *U.S. News & World Report.* 9 Oct. 1995. Print.

Gendreau, Paul, Claire Goggin, and Francis T. Cullen. "The Effects of Prison Sentences on Recidivism: User Report 1999–3." *Prison Policy Initiative.* 1993. Web.

Schwartz, B. and Steven J. Robbins. *Psychology of Learning and Behavior.* 4th ed. New York, NY: W. W. Norton & Company, 1995.

Schamalleger, Frank. *Criminal Justice Today: An Introductory Text for the 21ˢᵗ Century.* Upper Saddle River, NJ: Prentice-Hall, 1997.

United States Department of Justice. "Criminal Offender Statistics." *Bureau of Justice Statistics.* August 8, 2007. Web.

Summing Up

Persuasive essays give you a chance to present a claim and back it up with deductive (one point leading to the next) or inductive (extrapolating from data) reasoning. Readers consider the writer credible and sincere when opposing viewpoints are presented in a clear and fair manner, claims are reasonably stated, and the tone is balanced and logical. Combine logic and reasoning along with evidence and appeals to the reader's emotions and values. Fairly state and effectively refute counterarguments. Choose examples that are compelling, but also representative.

Persuasive essays include:

- Claims (the central claim is the thesis)

- Counterarguments fairly stated

- Refutations to counterarguments

- Deductive and/or inductive reasoning

- Unbiased, reliable, concise evidence and data, duly attributed

- Examples, if appropriate

- Appeals to reader's logic, emotions, values, etc.

Definition

The whole point of writing a definition essay is to draw attention to something unknown: a new word or phrase, a new connotation for a common word or phrase, a new audience for a revolutionary concept, a new insight into an existing concept. When these cannot be explained with a simple dictionary synonym, or if the synonym requires explaining, an essay is necessary. In writing your definition essay, avoid dictionary definitions and express the meaning in your own words.

Definition essays should include what the subject is *not* as well as what it is. Differentiate it from like concepts, explaining how it is similar, and how, in important ways, it is dissimilar. Near misses are often more crucial to explain than antithetical examples, so that the reader can identify the defining traits of the subject. If you can place your concept along a continuum, make sure to include the two extremes along with a clear appraisal of where your idea fits along that continuum.

As in any essay, examples help convince the reader that your assessment is right and fair. Include "textbook" examples as well as those that lie along the boundaries. Similes and metaphors also help to convey the traits of your concept. Just be sure to explain how they fit, so that they reader will correctly map the attributes from the metaphor to the subject.

You might want to start by drawing a concept map or Venn diagram, to identify boundaries, shared traits with similar concepts, and overlapping terminology. Then each paragraph can tackle one or more aspect of what the concept is or is not, and what is similar and not similar to it. Also consider, if relevant, what the word or phrase meant in the past and how and why it has appeared now or evolved over time.

Example:

> Parenthood is the most challenging job any adult can attempt. Whether or not this undertaking coexists with a "real" job, it is demanding, a 24-hour commitment. It requires brilliant decision-making (ballet or karate? bedtime hour? private school, or public?), 24-7 devotion (tummy aches at 2am, an essay postponed until the night before it's due), eternal optimism (the haircut *will* grow out, she *will* discover that boy is wrong for her), and endless energy. But any parent who thinks that sheer energy and right decisions will do the trick has missed the whole point of parenting: to let go. Let go? Ah yes, eventually! But when? How much, and how soon? Parenting as letting go is a day-to-day process that begins with the child's first tottering step. And it ends—never.

Summing Up

Write a definition essay for words or phrases that are commonly misunderstood or unknown. Avoid the dictionary (except to confirm your understanding) and use your own words, examples, and counterexamples. Consider the history of the concept and be sure to define the boundaries of the definition by describing what is not included in the definition and by comparing it to similar concepts that might be mistaken for it.

Definition essays can include:

- The origin of the concept

- What it is not

- What it is

- What it is like

- What it is not like

- Synonyms (also defined)

- Extreme and typical cases

- Examples

- Analogies

- No dictionary definitions

Comparison–Contrast

The point of writing a comparison-contrast essay (so-named to suggest that it covers both similarities—comparison—and differences—contrast) is not simply to list the similarities and differences, but to use them to make a larger point. To that end, analysis of your subjects will help you derive a thesis, which will state the point of the essay. The thesis might take some form of the following sample templates:

> All things considered, [subject A] is [value★] than [subject B] because *x*.

> Even though [concession], [subject A] is [value★] than [subject B] and therefore [suggested action]

> value★ will be a word or phrase such as: better, worse, stronger, more pervasive, more feasible, less dangerous, less costly, etc.

Sample comparison-contrast essay thesis statements:

> On the whole, bridge is harder than chess because there are more variables and more rules to remember.

Although the pay is low and the hours long, teaching is more rewarding that working in business because of the daily satisfaction of making a difference in young people's lives.

To analyze your comparison topic, start listing the traits necessary to compare. It might help to use a Venn diagram or a table to organize your thoughts.

Venn diagram:

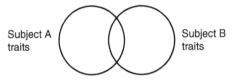

Subject A traits   Subject B traits

Table:

Trait	Subject A	Subject B

The very act of looking at your subjects in this way will help you decide not only what categories of traits to discuss but how to organize the essay. Generally, you will want to organize it point by point, rather than describing Subject A's traits and them Subject B's. This will prevent the essay from lapsing into a description of each, instead of making a true comparison. As you peruse your charts, deciding how to group and cluster the traits, consider how the relative strengths and weaknesses stack up. Some aspects are clearly more significant than others, and your essay will need to explain why this is so. Once you have completed a comparison assessment you can decide how to order the material. Here is one option:

Introduction

Trait 1

   How Subject A & B are similar
   How Subject A & B are different

Trait 2

   How Subject A & B are similar
   How Subject A & B are different

Trait 3

> How Subject A & B are similar
> How Subject A & B are different

Trait 4

> How Subject A & B are similar
> How Subject A & B are different

Etc. (more groups as needed)

Conclusion

Each trait (or group of similar traits) might comprise one or more paragraphs with similarities and differences together. Within the paragraph, certain kinds of sentences lend themselves to comparisons. For example, notice how tidily two characters in Mark Twain's novella *Pudd'nhead Wilson* are compared, using a sentence composed of two independent clauses joined by a semicolon:

> Luigi has a short temper, while Angelo is mild mannered; Luigi drinks, while Angelo is a teetotaler.

Parallel structure also serves nicely:

> Roxana, the black slave, is resourceful, smart, and principled, while her white counterpart, Rowena, is naïve, selfish, and simple-minded.

The key is to discover the traits that matter in discerning differences between Subject A and Subject B. Sometimes it makes sense to order your essay simply by presenting the first subject and all of its traits, then addressing the second subject. If you do so, though, be certain to discuss the same traits in each section:

Introduction

Subject A

> Trait 1
> Trait 2
> Trait 3

Subject B

Trait 1 as compared to Subject A
Trait 2 as compared to Subject A
Trait 3 as compared to Subject A

Conclusion

The second format works well for **then and now** essays, listing the traits under consideration in Subject A then comparing them in the section about Subject B. In effect, the Subject A section sets up the categories of comparison, while the Subject B paragraph makes the comparisons. This format would also suit an essay where you are making a proposal, such as a proposal to revise the exam week. Subject A would consist of what is wrong with the current situation (the status quo) and Subject B would propose the changes to be made.

Example: Comparing the Italian twins to Tom and Chambers in Mark Twain's *Pudd'nhead Wilson*.

In *Pudd'nhead Wilson,* Mark Twain explores the sensitive issue of nature versus nurture, through two pairs of characters: a set of biological twins and a pair of babies who resemble each other, and are switched at birth. The biological twins, Luigi and Angelo, share many common characteristics, such as excellent manners and good looks, yet they have distinctly different personalities and tastes. Luigi has a short temper, while Angelo is mild mannered; Luigi drinks, while Angelo is a teetotaler. Roxie creates another set of "twins" when she switches two babies—Tom (a white child) and Chambers (a black child)—at birth. She is able to do this because the so-called black child has only a trace of black blood, so they are physically indistinguishable. They have the opposite nurturing experience from what was expected, yet certain of their characteristics seem to persist despite their environment. Tom (formerly Chambers), raised into wealth and entitlement, fails to adopt the noblesse oblige expected of the elite class, raising questions about whether it is his black blood or social forces that turns him into a confirmed thief, liar, and murderer. Chambers (the former Tom), on the other hand, seems to adopt the subordinate submissiveness of slaves, but it is not clear whether his humility is a genetic tendency or an indication that a black person can have dignity despite his circumstances. A third set of "twins" emerges from the names of the two key women, Roxana and Rowena, one with an almost negligible amount of black blood that keeps her in the servant class, the other, genetically white. These two women also defy stereotyping, for Roxana, the black slave, is resourceful, smart, and principled, while her white counterpart, Rowena, is naïve, selfish, and simple-minded. By imbuing these pairs of cross-racial "twins" with unexpected characteristics, Twain succeeds in destabilizing the myth of genetic determination, suggesting that society can do better than consign a black child to a life of inferiority and degradation.

Summing Up

In comparison essays, the reader expects to see the subjects compared point by point, either serially (one at a time) or together. If you compare one and then the other, compare them on the same attributes, so that the reader sees how they line up against each other. The key to a successful comparison essay is plotting out the similarities and differences first, so that the essay is tightly and predictably structured. The thesis and conclusion should discuss why the differences and similarities matter. It helps to create a visual map so that you clarify your own thinking before you write your comparison.

Comparison-contrast essays include:

- Logical, predictable, structure

- Common, shared traits

- Dissimilarities

- Evidence

- A larger point (the thesis) made through the comparison

Cause–Effect

We live in a time of an unprecedented pace of change, with perhaps an even more unprecedented urge to explain the causes and consequences of those changes. As the world grows exponentially more complex, we face daily questions of cause and consequences regarding the safety, security, and vitality of the future: Has human activity compromised the environment? Will conservation efforts save endangered species? Can financial regulation prevent future economic disasters?

Cause-effect essays attempt to explain why a trend or event happened or what consequences will occur. They answer, "What happened or will happen?" and "Why?" Since the whole point of the essay is to describe causes and consequences behind events and trends, your analysis of the relative contribution of factors is key to the success of the essay. Writing such essays help you develop the problem-solving skills necessary to live in this complex world.

History teachers are quick to point out that most events do not result from a single cause, but from a number of contributing causes. Some may be necessary causes (the consequences could not have happened without this particular cause), some sufficient (possibly the sole cause), some long-term, some short-term. A proximate cause immediately precedes the outcome, and a catalyst might set events into motion. Causes might co-exist and converge to cause an outcome, or one cause may lead to an effect that becomes a cause in its own right, comprising a causal chain. Or, an accumulation of contributing causes might swell to a tipping point[1] after which there is no returning to a prior state. For example, when the Civil Rights Movement in the United States reached a tipping point of public awareness, the issue dominated every news medium and made it almost impossible for states to continue to resist implementing federal laws against racial discrimination. Determining which kinds of causes matter in your topic is the task of the analysis phase, which promises to be both a rewarding intellectual exercise and good practice in developing your critical-thinking and problem-solving skills.

To analyze cause and effects, look at the elements and events that precede and follow the consequence you are examining; i.e., look upstream as well as downstream. After listing your ideas, you may find it useful

---

1 Malcolm Gladwell defines "tipping point" as "the moment of critical mass, the threshold, the boiling point," when a movement towards change becomes impossible to avoid." (*The Tipping Point: How Little Things Can Make a Big Difference,* Little, Brown, 2000, p. 12).

to consider how the causes and effects can be mapped to best fit your findings. Here are three possible cause-effect formats:

The Fishbone Format:

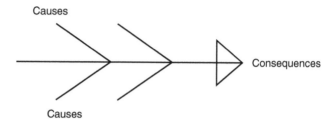

The Tributary Format:

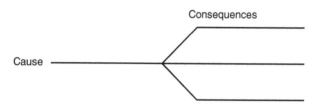

The Causal Chain:

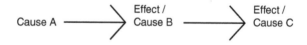

Once you settle on a conceptual map, look over your outline and evaluate your assumptions. Are all of the causes represented? Can some of them be grouped for efficiency? Test the validity of your mapping of cause and effect. You want to avoid certain pitfalls such as oversimplification, misattribution of causes that have no bearing or causative influence, or the logical fallacy of the *post hoc, ergo propter hoc* (following this, therefore caused by this), which mistakes sequence with causation. Also assess which causes are absolutely necessary and which are contributive, but not crucial. Can you identify a catalyst, something outside of the line of causation, that puts the wheels into motion? Consider, also, plausible alternatives that others consider pertinent but which you find unconvincing. You gain in credibility when you engage these issues seriously instead of ignoring or dismissing them.

When you begin to write, consider grouping like causes together into paragraphs. Topic sentences are easy: each will be a short statement of the nature of a cause or causal group. For example, one paragraph in an essay about the causes of the American Civil War might be headed by a topic sentence that claims:

> At the heart of the conflict was a debate over states' rights versus federal powers.

Along the way, define key terms and use plenty of examples, statistics, and other evidence to support your assessment. Provide a broad enough sample base; readers are rightly skeptical when conclusions are based on a single incident or a small number of cases. If this is a predicting essay, speculating about outcomes, be sure to address probability. Is the outcome inevitable (a tipping point has been reached), likely, or merely possible? For causal chains, explain how the outcome or effect of one cause can become a cause in its own right and use deductive reasoning to demonstrate how the stages are linked.

You may want to dispense with plausible alternatives in the beginning of the essay, before setting out your findings. Where you are uncertain, use tempering language to qualify your statements: "most likely," "seems" "might." Avoid overstating your case. Consider whether to build up to your most convincing evidence or to present it immediately, and be sure to explain each link of any causal chains. Your concluding paragraph usually will suggest a way forward—to extricate from or avoid an unwanted consequence or to assure a welcome one.

Example:

> The events that culminated in the American Revolution were myriad and complicated. Thus, the resulting rupture in relations was definitely not inevitable. Although scholars debate about how much each individual event contributed, the causes ultimately line up on two distinct sides: an ever increasing authoritarianism on the part of England, and an ever widening spirit of independence on the part of the loosely joined colonies.
>
> For England's part, the course was necessary. Taxes had to be levied to pay to protect the colonies, which, as they expanded, required more and more expensive military support and which failed to purchase as many English goods as hoped. One first attempt at control was to limit the westward movement of the colonists, with King George's 1763 proclamation forbidding the settlers to resettle beyond the Appalachian Mountain chain.

But financially, things were dire. The British debt had doubled after the French and Indian War. A series of new taxes aimed to recovering funds and the 1765 quartering act were designed to offset the cost of keeping troops fed in the far away colony. England felt it was taking measured, prudent steps to assure that it could protect and maintain the colonies and assure that trade relations would be productive for both sides.

At the same time, the colonies—though diverse in character, economic goals, religious views, and political interests—were developing a shared spirit of independence. These were the progeny of hardy settlers who had carved towns out of the wilderness, established laws, and required their peers to honor them. Furthermore, they were inspired by the English Bill of Rights, and felt that its covenants applied to them. The disparate colonies communicated through handbills and local printing endeavors. Therefore, it is no surprise that the Sons of Liberty, formed in 1765 to refute the Stamp Act, focused their efforts on printing and distributing angry responses to British insults to colonial autonomy. Their missives reached even the illiterate, as they were read aloud in taverns, inspiring lively debates. And each of the printed documents carried a sharp reminder of the Stamp Act, since printed material was the pipeline of communication, and every communiqué of the Sons of Liberty was "stamped" with a reminder of King George's imperious demands. The Stamp Act could not have been more offensive to colonial eyes, though it seemed like a simple and efficient solution to King George's financial concerns. Tempers reached a boiling point even though the Act was repealed a year later. The damage had already been done. When the colonists and the British troops clashed, therefore, the rage that was fomenting in the colonists erupted upon the spilling of the first blood. And with King George thousands of miles away, a diplomatic response was not in the offing. The shot heard round the world, though not inevitable, was certainly predictable.

Summing Up

Cause-effect essays require careful analysis to map causal relationships before writing, in order to produce an essay that is logical and easy to follow. The writer needs to consider how much the causes relate to each other, being careful not to oversimplify or to mistake events that simply *precede,* with events that actually *cause*. In describing causes, also address how much they impact the outcome, making a distinction between major and minor causes. Sometimes several smaller events add up to a larger consequence, so explain why they reached a tipping point, if that is what occurred.

Cause-effect essays include:

- Necessary, sufficient, and contributing causes, identified as such

- Long- and short-term causes, proximate causes, catalysts, and favorable conditions

- Assessment of probability and potential tipping points

- Organization by causal groups

- Consideration of plausible alternatives

- Definitions and evidence

- Deductive reasoning

- No oversimplification, overstatement, *post hoc, ergo propter hoc*, or other faulty reasoning

Explication

The purpose of writing an explication essay is to demonstrate your skills of interpretation. Usually, you will be asked to explicate a poem, a passage, a monologue, or scene—not an entire work—for explication by its very nature is an art of telescoping in and scrutinizing details in order to explain how they contribute to the meaning of the work as a whole. Yet even though you are addressing a part of a text, you must also explain what the whole piece is about, and what themes or large ideas it engages and explores.

The essay will be the account of your close analysis of a text, where the overall interpretation is the thesis and the body of the essay "shows your work" as you would do for a math proof. Your proof will focus on the significant details of the text, explaining each one. After annotating and drawing inferences from the text through analysis as described in Chapters 1 and 2, you should be able to identify a theme and then choose the interpretive elements that support your reading. Because an explication focuses minutely on how you see the meaning, the essay may proceed sequentially through the text, unpacking key phrases as you go, though it should be more robust than a simple line-by-line translation.

The difference between an explication essay and a persuasive one is that an explication focuses on *meaning*, such as identifying the meaning of Robert Frost's poem "The Road Not Taken" as the way in which one looks back on life decisions (an easily confirmable claim). A persuasive essay goes a step further and proposes a theory about the text that is more controversial and wider in scope. A persuasive essay might, for example, put this particular poem into a generalization about several Frost poems, suggesting that they reflect aspects of Frost's personal history. This type of persuasive essay telescopes *out* from the text and puts it into context or analyses it from the perspective of a critical view—feminism, Marxism, structuralism—or from a historical, biographical, or psychological one. A persuasive essay answers *Why* and *How* questions while an explication answers *That* the text means *x* or refers to *y* theme or idea.

An explication essay, then, starts with an interpretation that refers to a theme or large idea as its thesis, and continues by supporting that interpretation by citing the key phrases, unpacking them, and tying them to the thesis. Stay close to the source and fill the essay with plenty of quotations, allowing the text to speak for itself, with a little push of inference. The cited material should be fairly evenly distributed in the text, like chocolate chips in a cookie. Reading an explication should be like reading the original text with an alert and knowledgeable guide offering helpful insights along the way about the implication of the author's choice of imagery, diction, syntax, organization, and so on. Introductions and conclusions can be relatively straightforward, containing a brisk announcement of the meaning in the former and a tidy summing up of insights discovered in the latter.

Example:

> Shakespeare in Sonnet 30 presents a sorrow-laden narrator who pays tribute to a dear friend by describing how this friend can dispel his sadness. He offers this affirmation as a kind of summing up, placing his many sorrows on the negative side of a mental balance sheet with the friendship as the lone but offsetting entry in the other column.
>
> The narrator seems inclined to dwell in sorrow, to wallow in self-pity, almost as though he enjoys this state of mind, for he recalls his regrets and grievances during "sessions of <u>sweet</u> silent thought." Instead of daydreaming about the friend or loved one, he starts by daydreaming about all that has gone wrong

in his life: missed opportunities ("the lack of many a thing I sought"), wasted time ("my dear time's waste"), and lost loves ("love's long-since-cancelled woe"). He apparently has no accomplishments to post onto the accounting balance sheet. Instead, he morosely recalls losses that never diminish, paying the price of them in tears and sorrow, "as if not paid before." These seem the reflections of an older man looking back on a live not particularly well lived.

It is not until the final couplet that the reader sees any relief, and it comes about only "if" the narrator calls to mind his beloved friend. The final lines are simple, short, and at first seemingly inadequate in comparison the weight of the rest of the poem. Removed from the catalogue of sorrows by a separate, brief stanza, the idea of the friend is presented as a kind of magical thought that makes "all sorrows end," or vanish. Of course, the real losses are not "restored" as the couplet claims, but the narrator realizes that because of the friendship, his sorrows do not matter. It is not that the friend consoles the narrator, but that the idea of having the friend consoles and completes him, as the couplet completes the poem. Sonnet 30 ultimately valorizes the simple joy of companionship, a possession that outweighs everything else.

Summing Up

Explication essays are an account of your close analysis of a text, where you "show your work" and move from idea to idea or sequentially through the text, quoting liberally and explaining the implications of the lines as they relate to the larger themes and ideas presented. The content of your essay is *how* the text conveys its message and/or produces the effect it does.

To explicate a text, you must first spend time analyzing it rigorously. You will find that the more you work on it, the more layers you will uncover. When you write, however, proceed through the text, not through the evolution of your ideas.

Explication essays include:

- An interpretation of meaning, theme, main idea (what the text is *about*)

- Analysis of *how* the language and structure communicate the ideas

- Connotations and implications of key phrases and techniques
- Plenty of quoted evidence

Reflective

The purpose of writing a reflective essay is to demonstrate the depth and breadth of your thinking. The reflective essay can be less overtly structured than a persuasive or definition essay, yet it is not meant to ramble along without direction. Some of your reflections may digress, contradict each other, or fizzle out, but by the end of the reflection essay, the reader must feel that philosophical territory has been charted or discovered, and that insights have occurred.

As for other essays, preparing to write a reflective essay starts with productive brainstorming. The essay is not just a transcription of the brainstorming process, however. You'll want to put some shape to your ideas, and provide it with an appropriate, attention-getting introduction. The pace should be thoughtful and meditative; the tone frank, even humble. This is not the place to lecture your reader or to offer grand advice. Demonstrate your wisdom without attempting to impose it on your reader. The essay should be a window into your interior thinking process at your most honest and self-aware.

The essay can begin with a short description of a place, moment, or event that proved thought-provoking to you. Reconstruct the moment using a range of senses, using present tense, to drop your reader into the experience. Provide just enough context, including setting, characters, and the source of conflict to evoke a mood. Allow the reader to feel as though she is there with you, seeing and sensing the moment.

After the stage is set, begin the meditative section. This is where the concrete opens to the abstract. Perhaps you will ruminate about how things would differ now, had the moment not taken place. Or you may pose various interpretations of the event. Or the setting may launch seemingly unrelated reflections inspired by some aspect of the experience. For example, sitting in a bus station might lead to reflection about the growing divide between the rich and poor. Take the reader through the mental connections you make, arriving at their larger philosophical significance. Explore these layers in some depth, being careful not simply to repeat the same ideas in different words. Instead of circling around the same idea, ask yourself where it came from, what implications it has, what significance it holds.

The movement in a reflection essay proceeds somewhat like the tacking of a sailboat, shifting "side-to-side" as it goes forward, rather than charging directly towards a conclusion:

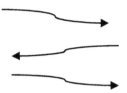

At the end, come back to the initial event or scene, now with greater understanding. To conclude, explain how the entire experience—the initial moment plus the reflections—has changed you. Possibly, you will express a resolution to alter your future behavior. In any event, your purpose is not to advise the reader but to share the advice you have given yourself.

Example:

Bad News

The earthquake had toppled half of an apartment building, exposing a rabbit warren of compartments of various decors. In one, the remains of an exquisite brocade drapery flaps in the morning breeze. In another, the clawed foot of a shabby couch hangs precipitously over the crumbled edge, a hand-knit afghan still stretched across its back. A patchwork palette of unharmonious colors: in the exposed rooms of one floor alone—a too-cheery pink, a tasteful celery green, a dull gold, four hues of blue. Paintings tilt dizzily—bizarre modern affairs, tacky reproductions, religious icons (this is Chile, after all, a catholic country), avante-garde photographs. Television hearth-gods preside with various sizes of empty gaze.

The camera pans to the ground to show a tangle of abandoned clothing, pots, pans, and plants. Here and there a torn family photo, a frayed dog collar, a broken fishbowl among fragments of plaster, concrete, and cracked tile. Nearby, a television crew interviews one of the survivors. The man smiles, impossibly, for his moment in the public eye. The well dressed journalist has just flown in from New York or Paris...somewhere untouched, but predatory with curiosity and something more—a sick hunger for the gruesome details.

What is this morbid curiosity? A whole industry thrives on it, responding to (creating?) the demand, the voyeuristic craving, for bad news. Who hasn't dwelled on the taped aftermath of chaos, or waited in breathless anticipation of, almost wishing for, a tsunami heading for Hawaii's luxury shoreline? And when will the coverage end? When the next big crisis appears, and we turn our morbid attention to some new ghastliness. Would it not more dignified, more caring, to announce the tragedy and focus on ways to help, rather than accept someone else's tragedy as a form of sick entertainment? I take one more glance at the carnage as I grab the remote and turn off the television. Maybe I can't change the news, but I can certainly change my viewing habits.

Summing Up

Reflective essays take the reader through an experience that led to reflective thought and insight, sparked by some external event that, by the close of the piece, appears differently due to the change in heart that has occurred. Do not simply ramble, but free-write first and then create a structure that allows you to link your insights to an object or experience that inspired you. Starting and ending with that object or experience creates an artful essay.

Reflective essays include:

- A description of an inspiring scene or event

- Alternative interpretations of the experience

- A meditative pace

- Philosophical musings

- An explanation of the significance of the experience

- A return to the original scene or event, with new wisdom

Descriptive

A descriptive essay paints a portrait in words. Its purpose is to bring to life, on the page, an event, experience, person, place, or process. Descriptive essays go by a variety of different names: expository (which "exposes" a topic through description), narration (which tells a brief anecdote or story), description (which evokes a mood through a description of a place), process analysis (which tells how to do something, step by step).

In each of these, the overriding goal is to convey a controlling idea or to evoke a mood. For example, a description of a cabin in the woods could evoke homespun independence, or abject poverty; a process analysis can convey the necessity for careful attention or the satisfaction of becoming mesmerized by the steps of a task.

In a **descriptive essay** about a place, the narrative should proceed spatially, panning from top to bottom, from the door to an inner sanctum, from a zoomed-out global view to a zoomed-in close-up. The reader needs a sense of location and direction in space and will become confused by narration that jumps from one spot to another too abruptly. In descriptions of space, transitions words consist of directional cues: above, below, beside, inside, surrounding, etc.

A **process analysis essay** proceeds step-by-step but it need not be presented as a relentless list of tasks: this, then that, then the next. If possible, group steps into stages or classes of steps: for example, the preparation, assembly of materials, the roll-out, the follow-up. A process analysis also requires a controlling idea, such as the need for focus, flexibility, or appreciation for the arduousness of the task.

A **narrative essay** relates an anecdote. Here it is important to include the telling details, the textures of experience that allow the reader to sense and feel the experience through evocative description, imagery, and figurative language. Your goal is to take the reader to the moment and steep him in the experience. Be aware of details or modifiers that confuse, derail, or contradict the mood or idea you hope to produce, being mindful of connotations as well as denotations in selecting precise and pertinent vocabulary. Transitional words should move the narrative along: first, then, later, before, after, when, finally, etc.

An **exposition essay** "exposes" an idea or thing to the view of the reader. You need to have a reason for your exposé—to reveal an uncommonly known or misunderstood truth. Here the "story" consists of the facts and implications that make the topic worthy of note. You are describing a state or change of state that deserves attention, so highlight the crucial aspects through your description. This is the classic format for investigative journalism. For example, your exposition essay might reveal how a particular factory is secretly dumping toxic waste. Rather than simply declaring this outright, your essay can evoke the place of damage, perhaps accompanied by chillingly insensitive comments from the managers of the factory.

Note: descriptive essays differ from reflective essays in one key way: in descriptive essays, the writer focuses on the thing described, so the majority of the essay describes it. The controlling idea is central, is evoked, but not elaborated at length. Alternatively, the reflective essay begins with a brief description, but spends most of the time reflecting on the ideas that evolve from it.

Example Descriptive Essay:

As a prerequisite to a pathology internship at a local hospital my junior year of college, my roommate and I arrived at the local morgue at 8:00 AM on a Saturday to observe an autopsy. We had joked about throwing up into our breast pockets or fainting into a gaping thoracic cavity, but I hadn't really considered how disquieting the experience would prove to be. The assistant to the medical examiner was late, so when I failed to offer any semblance of assistance, my roommate (who was president of the Powerlifting team at school) stepped to the other side of the woman and effortlessly ushered her to the autopsy table. I stepped back, focused on my shoelaces, and hoped nothing more would be asked of me.

This first case was a 500-pound methamphetamine overdose. I braced myself for the grisly horror of her disembowelment. The examiner lifted his scalpel and set to his work. As her large organs slipped out of latexed hands, sliding on the stainless steel, I felt not the nausea and revulsion I expected, but a clouded eeriness. The liver, yielding to the expertise of the pathologist's blade, unfurled into a blossom of slick, sectioned tissue. Scar tissue, chronic disease, and evidence of her drug abuse were identified in the inner sanctums of her body. The process was earnestly narrated by the elderly medical examiner, but I floated above the carnage, not fully engaging what was happening. A radio in the back of the room was tuned to an oldies station, and the melodies of my parents' childhoods imbued the autopsies with a creepiness that I can't fully verbalize. As he sorted through her twisting, glossy organs like a CPA flipping through tax reports, I winced at the gloom of his job, at the bleakness of my future. We dutifully catalogued the features of her disease, and we dutifully recorded them in our burgeoning notebooks. Then my roommate deftly slid the overdose (as we called her) onto a cold steel gurney and slid her into the cadaver cooler. My initiation into death was over. Hers was, too.

On the way back to campus, I tuned out my roommate's voice as he rehashed the details of what we had seen that day. He was starting his pathology internship the following Monday, and was mulling over the different scheduling options. H sounded like a pathology addict. One fix was definitely not enough. But for me, it was plenty.

Summing Up

Descriptive essays paint a portrait in words that evokes a mood, whether they describe a person, place, or process. Employ a narrative strategy, such as moving through time (past, present, future) or through space (top to bottom, west to east) or through stages (preparation, assembly, testing, deployment) to convey the material in a way that invites the reader to explore the content, using directional transition words and phrases to guide the reader through the experience.

Descriptive essays include:

- A portrait in words
- Can be one of several types: spatial description, process analysis, narration, exposition
- Transition words and phrases that map the experience
- A controlling idea or an evocation of a particular mood
- Carefully chosen details that contribute to the impact of the whole
- Analogies and metaphors that help to organize the material
- Vivid imagery and similes or metaphors
- Sensory details

Classification

Classification appeals to our natural inclination to sort ideas and things into categories. We classify whenever we write: when organizing an analytical essay, for example, we sort examples into categories that become body paragraphs. Outlines consist of the categories and sub-categories of the topic. An essay that foregrounds the categories themselves is a classification essay. For example, you might want to list and assess types of fuel-efficient cars, or to make distinctions between various types of exoskeletal organisms. Your overriding goal is justify your choice of categories for a particular group of items, and to convince the reader that your classification structures the material thoroughly and fairly.

To create categories, you will need some kind of organizing principle so that you have clear criteria for separating one example from another, based on their qualities. This will be the thesis statement of the essay. For example, to classify dogs, you might choose categories of size or of temperament. Often the organizing principle is a matter of increasing degree, from a small to a large amount of some quality. Other typical organizing principles include location (urban, suburban, rural) or type (social, political economic) or time (past, present, future). Be sure to not to leave out an important category or your essay will seem incomplete. Use parallel structure to list the categories as this assures that you are separating them on a legitimate criterion.

Once you derive your categories, organizing the essay is simple: usually you will want to progress "up the line" in terms of degree, or start with the least and move to the most important category, each perhaps comprising its own body paragraph. Describe how each category differs, what qualities are unique to it, while connecting them to the overall group. Consider subcategories as well and provide typical examples of each one. Your conclusion should express why it is important to recognize the categories as separate rather than lumping them all together and to underscore the reason for looking at the topic afresh.

Example:

> There are three main types of popular fiction that concern themselves with murder, death and dying: horror, ghost, and gothic fiction. Each of these separate categories of "death fiction" holds a distinctly different relationship to the here and now. In horror fiction, the threat enters into the everyday world, the here and now, wreaking havoc through bloody dismemberment and murder. Horror fiction inspires a particular type of fear—from the realization that a physical attack could come at any time. In ghost fiction, the action happens in a surreal place, a place on the border between the here and now and the afterlife, as the dead return to

the world of the living and attempt to contact them. Ghost fiction inspires a different type of fear, one that is existential and spiritual, deriving from the idea that the sacred boundary between life and death has become porous. In gothic fiction the reader enters a different world that exists in a "pocket" of the here and now—in an old, decrepit castle, in a crypt, a graveyard, or some other confined space—where the characters must contend with a bizarre new set of physics and rules. The fear inspired by gothic fiction consists of psychological horror, the fear that familiar scientific principles and logic no longer apply. In all three, the goal is to escape from a place of possible death and return to reality.

Summing Up

Classification essays sort material in a designated group into categories according to some guiding principle selected by the writer. Categories consist of features that separate or distinguish individuals within a group, such as types of teachers, sizes of balloon, shapes of shells. The essay can proceed from one category to the next, explaining what identifies each particular classification from the others.

Classification essays include:

- A thesis that states the organizing principle
- A reason for examining the topic
- An inclusive list of categories and their unique, identifying qualities
- Defining characteristics
- Examples

Précis (Summary)

The purpose of writing a précis is to demonstrate your ability to capture the essence of an original text, usually a scholarly article, but sometimes a work of literature. It is a valuable exercise, as it requires you to understand the original text thoroughly, fathoming all of its complexities and putting them into your own words.

A précis is not a paraphrase; a paraphrase is a translation into your own words, and approximately matches the original in length. A précis must also be in your own words, but it distills the original to a fraction, perhaps 20% of its original length. Write in full sentences, using present tense. The thesis consists of a statement that defines the author's main idea.

Do not simply copy the author's words replacing a word here and there. Phrase the material in your own words, being careful not to allow the wording of the original slip into your version as though these are your own words, or you will have plagiarized the material. Also, do not simply proceed chronologically through the text. Instead, identify the main ideas and present them concisely, yet thoroughly. By the time you finish, you will have read the original text through several times. A good précis is itself a work of art, so choose your words carefully and honor the original by expressing its ideas in your own eloquent phrasing, including key phrases from the author in quotation marks. Since only one article is referenced, parenthetical citations can be omitted.

While the format of a précis can vary, here is one format that can serve as a guide. The first sentence should include the author's name, the title and date of the work, the genre (journal article, magazine article, book review, etc.) followed by a rhetorically accurate verb (claims, argues, suggests, asserts, proves, challenges, etc.) and a THAT clause containing the main idea or thesis of the work. Next, define the author's purpose and methods. It may take several sentences to describe what the author DOES to prove her point (offers examples, analogies, present testimonials, statistics, etc.). Include an example of the most compelling evidence, and be sure to quote responsibly. Include key terms and phrases. Finally, describe the intended audience or the relationship the author establishes with the audience as well as any bias that is revealed.

Example:

> In psychologist Steven Pinker's 2009 article "My Genome, My Self," he asserts that the future promise of genome testing is a mixed bag. On one hand, this genetic information could offer the opportunity to personalize medicine and reduce disease; on the other hand, however, he notes that those tested are liable to be "whipsawed by contradictory studies" about what the genome information really means, since hundreds of genes contribute to a single propensity. He starts with the personal example of getting his own genomes analyzed, which suggested that he has an 80% chance of becoming bald (he has a full head of hair and finds this unlikely) and a 12.6% chance of getting prostate cancer. He

quips that knowledge such as this "opens up a niche for bottom-feeding companies to terrify hypochondriacs by turning dubious probabilities into Genes of Doom." He then evaluates the current thinking on biological determinism versus environmental influence and concludes that both affect an individual's life. His purpose is to clarify that genome testing, which eventually may be able to predict tendencies even for such things as "trust and commitment, or a tendency to antisocial outbursts" is far from being a reliable tool for prediction or medication. He is writing for an educated audience, some of whom might be willing to pay anywhere from $399 for a small sampling to $99,500 for a more extensive sequence analysis. He notes that it would be prohibitively expensive to scan one's entire genome system, which would require a multi-gigabyte file. Although he acknowledges that genome information will be and is valuable, "the sheer complexity of the self will mean that it will not serve as an oracle on what the person will do."

Steven Pinker. "My Genome, My Self." *The New York Times*, January 11, 2009.

Summing Up

A précis is a structured summary of a longer piece, condensing it to a fraction of its full length while conveying its core ideas and key phrases. The thesis of the précis is the thesis of the original article. Important examples can be included as well. Be sure to identify the author's purpose and the intended audience. The précis writer does not evaluate or add personal information to the summary.

A précis includes:

- Thesis statement with the author name, title, genre, date and main idea

- A brief summary of the methods of proving the idea (statistics, anecdotes, etc.)

- Verbs in present tense

- Description of intended audience

- Assessment of bias

- Key words and phrases, quoted

Exam

The goal of writing an exam essay is to demonstrate your mastery of the concepts and principles of a course. It is not an exercise in reciting *what* you know as much as it is an exercise in showing how well you understand the subject. Your essay should foreground your insights into the concepts of the subject, effectively supported with examples and evidence from the readings. It must also answer the question posed—not sidestepping it or substituting an easier question—with eloquence and confidence.

After considering the nature of the exam question and what it asks you to do (see Analyzing Exam Questions, p. 33), create a scratch outline, recalling your practice outline on the topic. If parts of it do not come to mind immediately, continue on. Your mind will produce the information when you start writing. If you are stuck, take a few minutes to free-write. This will relax you and will probably lead to discovering an important insight. In your outline, list pertinent and typical examples. If the exam requires an explication of a text, annotate the text first, then prepare an outline based on your annotations. Choose the strongest evidence, that which is supported by other evidence in the text. In interpreting literature, remember the "rule of three" that suggests validating your interpretation by finding three places in the poem or story that support your reading. You cannot base, for example, a feminist or a Marxist reading on a single line.

Exam introductions should be brief and very much to the point. This is not the place for long introductions—just efficiently lead up to your thesis. Often you can construct a thesis simply by converting the question to a declarative sentence and then adding a completer such as "because," "proving," "suggesting," etc. Other times, you will have the leeway to construct your own thesis, and you should always take this opportunity to demonstrate your creativity under pressure. Your very first sentence, whether a brief attention-getter or the thesis itself, does something besides govern the content of the essay—it establishes your ethos as a writer. Since you want to make a good first impression, take some time to fashion an elegant first sentence. If the means to do so eludes you at first, leave a blank line or two so that you can come back to it later.

As you proceed to the body of the essay, keep in mind a few important pointers: develop ideas fully, provide examples in as much detail as possible, and write just enough to prove your point. Leave out details that are merely interesting but not critical, especially if they drift off topic. Link each piece of evidence back to the thesis by explaining *why* it proves your point. Use short, pithy quotations, properly cited. If your prompt is a text, include just the gist of the lines, an abbreviation of what you would include in a non-timed paper. Avoid wasting time and space copying out lengthy passages as your reader is no doubt familiar with the material and does not need the entire passage. Do not, however, simply refer to line numbers, forcing the reader back to the text to verify what you have chosen. Furthermore, do not simply "plop" the quotation into the essay, expecting the reader to make the necessary grammatical and contextual adjustments. Trim the passage to just the words you need and make them flow within your sentence. Cite quoted material responsibly, but efficiently, by abbreviating titles and names. Finally, make sure that your analysis "goes somewhere." Be vigilant about not circling around and around, simply repeating the same idea in different words. At the same time, be careful not to let the evidence take over the essay; your own ideas should be paramount, with the evidence there to prove it.

Finish with a concise, efficient closing sentence or two that states your final insight clearly, without over-dramatizing it. Avoid grand moralizations and lofty send-offs, but do show your reader the wider implications of the ideas you have explained.

Example:

Describe and analyze the differences in the ways in which artists and writers portrayed the individual during the Italian Renaissance and the Romantic era of the late eighteenth and early nineteenth centuries.

Intellectual movements have traced a zigzag pattern across history, each subsequent school of thought presenting an antithesis to its predecessor in some fashion. The Italian Renaissance served to shift the intellectual focus from the glory of God to the glory of the individual. Romantic thought, which arose nearly four centuries later, was the first to break the intellectual trend of individualism and shift the focus back away from each individual to people as a whole.

The Renaissance was the antithesis to medieval beliefs, which focused on God rather than individuals. Renaissance art, while necessarily clinging to religious themes, started a trend of highlighting the beauty of the human form. This incipient individualism perhaps is best seen in sculptures like Michelangelo's *Pieta*. While it is religious in nature as it depicts Mary holding Jesus after he is removed from the Cross, it glorifies the humanity—not the deity—in the body of Christ. The style of the sculpture is moreover derived from Greek and Roman art, thereby paying homage to *man's* great (pagan!) civilizations. The writing of the time also reflects this changed world view. Letters and manuscripts of the Italian Renaissance revel in the talent of men like Leonardo Da Vinci, although noting, almost as an aside, that his gifts were bestowed by God. In this way, the writers and artists of the Italian Renaissance began to recognize the value of the individual, forever changing the social, religious, and political path of Europe.

While each intellectual movement is a response to the next, the trend of individualism begun by the Renaissance was so strong that it was not until the late eighteenth century that Europe was met with an antithesis to this world view. This is not to say that Romanticism sought to devalue the individual, but rather that the Romantics bestowed value on the individual based on non-individualistic factors. Romantics took the unique soul of human-beings and replaced it with the more communal soil. Instead of glorifying talent, for example, Romanticism glorified blood and national identity. Part of the reason that Romanticism can be seen as the converse of the Renaissance is that Romantic thought harkened back to the Middle Ages. Just as medieval art focused on religious subjects (and considered the human form to be corrupted by sin), Romantic art depicted nature as the glorified source human identity. The literature of the Romantic era also downplayed individuality by constructing archetypical characters that typified cultural values. A perfect illustration of this is *Ivanhoe*, which tells idealistic tales of a medieval knight. This famous piece of literature combines all aspects of the Romantic era, from its nostalgia, to its emphasis on honor, to its blatant anti-Semitism.

When Hegel, a Romantic philosopher, examined the historical intellectual process of constructing a thesis and an antithesis, he developed a theory that all historical progress would converge on a great synthesis—that man was developing a Spirit that would work towards complete consciousness and understanding. What Hegel hit upon was the observation that history is not stagnant, not a ping pong ball bouncing back and forth between two world views, going nowhere. No, as each intellectual movement responds to the next, it also builds upon its predecessor's ideas. The men of the Renaissance did not simply reject religion, but used it to justify their admiration of God's creation, man. Similarly, the Romantics did not simply revert back to the Middle Ages, but instead took individualism and attempted to construct a theory by divining what made the individual so valuable. Thus, the relationship between the two views of the individual is not simply one of complete opposites, but of contrasts and developments.

Summing Up

To write a strong exam essay, first clarify what the question asks you to do. Then identify fitting examples and write a rough outline, including references to core concepts from the class. Answer in depth, with minimal introduction and minimal distractions. Be sure to include a few important examples and explain them thoroughly. Use lists to convey a lot of material quickly. Make sure that you answer the question, which may be expressed as a declarative form of the question, followed by "because," and the answer. This would be the thesis.

Exam essays include:

- A strong, elegant opening sentence
- A concise, direct introduction
- A thesis that answers the question
- Connections to core principles explored in the course
- Pertinent, pithy, properly cited evidence and/or examples
- Fully developed analysis
- An efficient conclusion that alludes to wider implications

Research

A research essay assignment asks not simply whether you can retrieve and present information but whether you can synthesize opposing information and interpretations into a coherent, compelling thesis. Thus the goal is not to report information but to demonstrate understanding of the implications of it at the deepest possible level. Even better is to demonstrate your ability to navigate between the various opinions on the topic while articulating your own clear opinion on it.

Your task begins with retrieving information, unless the essay will be based on documents provided to you, such as the AP English Language synthesis question or AP History document-based questions, for example. For these, follow roughly the same guidelines as for a research essay, trying to reach a thesis that is a bit beyond the obvious choices that most of the other test takers will reach. To make research as efficient as possible, begin with a guiding question or questions, usually of the What, How, or Why variety:

- What role does Catholicism play in the literature of Flannery O'Connor?

- How did the decision not to marry affect Queen Elizabeth I's reign?

- Why did Cuba turn toward communism after Fidel Castro's 1959 revolution?

A guiding question will focus your reading and help you decide which resources to keep and which to set aside. At first, read general introductions, such as encyclopedia entries, to give you a broad view of the topic. A soon as you can, start a scratch concept map that will help you place the large categories of information in relation to each other.

Example concept map: Cuba's turn toward communism

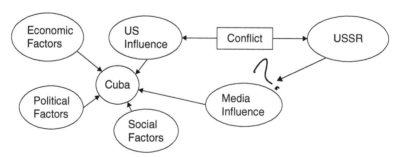

Next, identify sources. You'll want primary sources (sources from the time period or by the author under study) as well as secondary sources (interpretations and commentary on primary sources), with a good range of different opinions on the topic. Keep a list of possible texts, perhaps a copy of your library catalogue search, crossing out the ones you decide not to use. Find journal and magazine sources as well as books and use web sites as long as they are reliable (the site will remain active) and authoritative (produced by a legitimate author). Thus blogs can be a legitimate source if the blogger is reputable and keeps the blog up to date.

Remember that your own ideas should be in the foreground—the sources should bolster your arguments, not take over the essay. Most of your references should be primary documents, with only a few secondary ones, in a ratio something like this:

Your Ideas

Primary Sources

Secondary Sources

To find journal and magazine articles search a library online database. Learn how to use the advanced search function to select desirable date ranges, and to narrow your search. If you can, save the full text of sources as files, name them meaningfully (author last name, article title, abbreviated) and place them in a separate computer folder for research items.

As you review sources, ask yourself: is it comprehensive (does it cover the topic fully)? Is it balanced (not biased or overstated)? Is it sufficient (does it leave out important aspects)? Are the examples pertinent and typical?

Read purposefully and skim until you find what you need to support your thesis. Spend about five minutes assessing each resource. Look at the chapter titles, skip to the chapter with the most promising title, and read the first sentence of several paragraphs. If this source looks useful, read several paragraphs to make sure you can understand it. Flip through the book to find relevant tables or charts (use the table of illustrations at the front of the book). Check the index for specific topics, too. Ask yourself, does this resource contribute to my understanding? Stack promising books in one stack and return the rest.

Read critically, fitting each reading into a growing landscape of understanding. Update your concept map and your working thesis as your ideas evolve. Be careful that your reading does not shift you into a different topic and that you stay focused on mining each source for material; catch yourself if you lapse into passive reading.

Since the goal is to demonstrate your understanding of the deep implications of your topic and thesis, put yourself into a "conversation" with the sources. Think of a dinner party where each school of thought is represented by one interesting dinner guest. You are at the head of the table, asking questions and consolidating your understanding, while noticing that you agree with guest *A* (who may represent one or more reading in your research stack), and that you disagree with guest *B*, in some degree. The point of this analogy is to take you out of the mode of data-gatherer and into the mode of theory formulator, processing sources as a conversationalist or as someone making an important decision who grasps the essential information quickly.

See Chapter 1.2 on Note-Taking for guidelines on efficient researching.

Once you have finished taking notes, look over your thesis and concept map again to assure that you have researched enough. Firm up the thesis as needed, and then start coding passages according to conceptual groups. Sort citations into separate groups for each category. Some categories will need further subdivision, while others may be combined. Create an outline from this process and check it for completeness. Also check that you have enough evidence for each outline item. If not, more research may be necessary. See the chapters on Preparing to Write (3) and Getting Out the First Draft (5) for further guidance.

With a full outline, you may begin writing. Start with the group that is easiest to write—you don't have to start at the beginning. (See Body Paragraphs, Chapter 4.3.) As you work, integrate quotations into your sentences to make them flow smoothly with your ideas. Trim longer quotations down to the shortest, pithiest parts and introduce the author's name along with her title or discipline ("Prime Minister Putin," "sociologist Clifford Geertz," "moral philosopher Martha Nussbaum"). For quotations of four lines or more, indent the entire block, do not use quotation marks, introduce it with a colon (:), and put the citation at the end of the block:

> The people continued to be elated. Castro spoke practically every week on television, and was followed in his travels by representatives of all the media. His speeches were often made without warning, and lasted for many hours, upsetting the usual schedule of programs. Those in power were constantly in the news and the country was being rocked by the ongoing changes: the Rent Laws, the Agrarian Reform, the Tax Reform, the military trials of those accused of

committing genocide during the Batista regime; the efforts of the various revolutionary organizations. (Victoria 231)

As you write, make sure that the quoted material does not take over the essay. Keep your own voice uppermost. This is especially significant at the end of paragraphs, where you should end not with a quotation but your own words.

See the Appendix for a Political Science research essay.

Summing Up

A research essay asks you to synthesize your findings from the sources, to enter into a conversation with their ideas, and to present your findings in an organized and compelling essay that responsibly acknowledges source material. The key to success is to keep your research question in front of you as you look at sources and to keep track of your own words and those of others. Read deliberately, skimming through the material until you find what you need. Revise your thesis as new information enhances your understanding.

Research essays include:

- A theoretical synthesis of ideas that is more than a collection of facts

- Your own ideas in "conversation" with the sources

- A thesis that grows out of research

- Responsibly cited sources

- Carefully selected quotations, trimmed to fit your sentences

- A mix of reliable primary and secondary sources

- A formal, businesslike tone that avoids colloquialisms and "I" statements

4.2   Introductions

If you were taught the "funnel" approach to an introduction (start with general information and narrow down to your topic), it's time to advance to more intriguing methods, not least because the funnel introduction can entice you to start writing before you are ready. Instead of a funnel, think of the introduction as a kind of stage design, setting up your reader's expectations and foregrounding the thesis statement that will take center stage as the introduction comes to a close. Avoid sweeping, "panoramic" introductions that give little clue as to your topic, such as any version of, "Since the dawn of time…" Give just enough information to pique your reader's curiosity and to commit to satisfy that curiosity in the body of the essay. The introduction should be no broader than the topic of the thesis; it's like a door opening to a specific room.

The lead, or first, sentence can take various forms, as long as it is fresh and captivating, directing the reader's attention to a legitimate idea or concern. Avoid trite or overused leads, such as the much-abused dictionary definition, the easily-dismissed rhetorical question ("Have you ever thought about…?"), or the tired generalization ("Humans have gone to war throughout the ages."). Instead, consider starting with a:

- surprising fact or statistic (With xx% of motorists on the highways uninsured …)

- pertinent and concise quotation (Francis Bacon believed that "the best preservative to keep the mind in health is the faithful admonition of a friend.")

- short, relevant anecdote (Sentry duty for soldiers was so demanding and so crucial that during World War I getting caught asleep on sentry duty could be punished by death by firing squad. Today, however, some troops are vigilantly guarded by an ever-wakeful sentry robot.)

- paradox or enigma central to the topic (The shocking thing about advertisements is not how far they go but how little we react to them.)

- fair statement of the viewpoint you will oppose (Since the 18th century, economists have believed a free market is best for economic growth. However, the 2008 worldwide stock market crash has begun to convince some economists that only through strict regulation can a sustainable economy be maintained.)

- definition (in your own words) that lies at the heart of the topic (A failed state is a nation that no longer controls is military, its economy, or its future.)

- pithy, capsulizing statement (No one deserves to go without healthcare.)

Your aim is to delight the reader, intriguing him to read on. But also be mindful that the lead, or first, sentence sets the tone of the piece and hints at the scope. A lead that is wonderful on its own might not match the mood of the essay you are writing and thus, could mislead the reader. Once you settle on a lead, elaborate or qualify it as needed. The next several sentences escort the reader unambiguously to the thesis, if your essay requires one. These sentences set the stage, with pertinent, necessary background information establishing context and the common ground that prepares the reader to accept the thesis. Here, too, you can introduce core concepts that you will address. To do so, you will want to have settled on the main terms you will use to explore your topic. Ralph Waldo Emerson declared that in writing "three or four stubborn necessary words are the pith and fate of the business…the rest is circumstance, satellite, and flourish."[2]

Emerson suggests that the time spent up front identifying those core words will pay off in a clear, focused essay. Likewise, the thesis of any essay rests on three to five key terms, which can be introduced immediately. These key terms will provide coherence when they appear again in the body paragraphs. The sentences of the introduction must be tightly linked, each one leading logically to the next. By the time the thesis statement is reached, it should not be surprising, but inevitable.

Throughout the essay, but especially in the introduction, be forthright with your reader. Your position or opinion should be apparent, though not stated outright. Show respect to the reader by scrupulously staying on topic, leaving tangential issues to another essay, another day. The introduction is the reader's guide to the rest of the essay, so you may also want to preview what is to come by stating the main areas of analysis you will pursue.

Not all essay introductions state a thesis in the introduction, however. Some essays do not start with a thesis but rather build toward one, starting instead with a clear presentation of the problem to be discussed. The thesis will come at the end, having examined multiple options along the way. Here, too, the introduction serves to limit the scope of inquiry so that the essay is not so broad that any musings will fit.

Introductions to most essays should be brief, and exam essays introductions especially should be minimal, offering just enough to establish your credibility and make your thesis stand out from the crowd. The essay

---

2 *Journals and Miscellaneous Notebooks* 9:46, 250, Richardson 203.

question itself can be turned into the thesis, so, in effect, the introduction can consist of as little as two compelling sentences: the lead and the thesis. It's always a good idea, too, to charge up the thesis with more energy by stating it in imperative terms— x would be devastating, farcical, or morally wrong, or y is imperative, crucial, or inevitable. Your essay should be strong, with power emanating from the first sentence.

The thesis statement is one clear sentence that serves as the heart of the introduction and of the essay. You should have developed a thesis statement during your analysis of the topic (see chapter 3.3, Devising a Thesis) but here are a few reminders. First and foremost, the thesis must be an arguable statement, one with which an informed person could disagree. If everyone would agree with your thesis, what you have is an observation, not a thesis. It must also be provable, or the rest of the essay is going to be too difficult to write. It should be specific enough for the length of your paper and it should answer a "why" or "how" question. A good thesis statement also reveals your attitude, as shown through your choice of phrasing. It takes a stand, and possibly alludes to any major objections.

Example thesis statements:

- Even though plastics cause harm to the environment, their benefits to society far outweigh their recycling costs.

- Ammonite suture development demonstrates that progressive change in an attribute of a species, even when it benefits the species, is not necessarily the result of natural selection.

- While Plato's Republic illustrates many of the traits of an ideal society, it will never come into being because it ignores certain key aspects of human nature.

- Tim O'Brien's *The Things They Carried* is not a war story, but a post-war story: the story of the writer on a spiritual journey to find meaning and purpose in his memories of the Vietnam War.

While we're at it, let's look at some inadequate thesis statements and why they are not suitable:

- World War I caused millions of deaths and did not fully solve the international conflicts that caused it.

   ○ Too broad, not arguable. Doesn't take a stand.

- India has the power to supersede all of the current international hegemons.

  - Good topic, arguable, but doesn't specify what topic the essay will focus on.

- Wikileaks demonstrates that national leaders can be irrational and unethical.

  - This one takes a stand, but it's too obvious, not worth proving.

- In his novel, *The Things They Carried*, Tim O'Brien masterfully utilizes language to recreate war experiences and, as a result, the reader is able to feel how the soldiers felt while they were in Vietnam.

  - Not interesting and not arguable. And the word "masterfully" sounds pretentious.

- From the early 1600s to the 1900s, the Indian image has drastically changed.

  - This sounds more a topic sentence, and it's too obvious.

- The stereotyping of Indians transforms over time as social values change.

  - Actually, not bad! Could be improved by adding a phrase about how or why it changed.

Sample Introductions:

> The criminal justice system aims to accomplish three things: to punish and reform criminals by taking away the freedoms and privileges of citizenship, to make the streets safer by incarcerating criminals, and to deter future crime by demonstrating the cost of criminal behavior. However, the imprisonment of criminals does not succeed in meeting the goals hoped for by society. Our prisons burgeon with inmates and costs are skyrocketing, but too often imprisoned criminals come back to society more likely than before to commit further crimes.

> "I'm all in" roared the drunk at the blackjack table, "I'm all in." Placing 500 chips in the center of the table, the inebriated man sporting a purple silk bowling shirt blended well with the eclectic cacophony known as Vegas. To the bewilderment of onlookers, he proceeded to split a pair of tens and rake in several

thousand dollars in a matter of minutes. How was this possible? Easy: card counting. The drunk was actually quite sober, one of a group of MIT students who had set a goal to make over a million dollars in six months through gambling, and he made it. Was his success ethical?

Luisel Ramos, a Uruguayan model, died due to heart failure, a side effect of anorexia nervosa. She was 22, 5'9", and weighed just over 98 pounds. Her BMI or Body Mass Index was 14.5. A BMI of 16 is considered starvation, 18 is malnourished, and 20 is healthy. Ramos' death caused the Madrid Fashion Week to change their weight restrictions: now all models must have a BMI of at least 18 to walk the runway. But the fashion industry still drives too many young women into life-threatening eating habits.

Post World War I America reached a new level of wealth, affluence, amorality, and debauchery. As a successful man embroiled in these times, F. Scott Fitzgerald witnessed the moral bankruptcy of the contemporary "High Society," and reported on it, while maintaining his social standing at the heart of the social elite as well as participating in its moral bankruptcy. No wonder, then, that his novel *The Great Gatsby* both execrates and celebrates the vacuity and materialism of his era.

Summing Up

Your introduction sets the stage for the essay to come, so start with a clear and elegant, attention-grabbing lead-in, a concise and arguable thesis, and just enough elaboration to establish what you mean. Also introduce key terms and preview the major sections of the essay. However, the introduction should not be lengthy, nor should it get into the details of the essay. Save that information for later. The introduction is a "handshake" between you and the reader that clearly reveals what the reader will learn.

A good introduction includes:

• A lead that demonstrates that the topic is interesting and valuable

• A tone and style that establish the writer's ethos and eloquence

- Relevant context (brief background, title, author, as relevant)

- The scope of the topic or problem and a clear position on it (thesis)

- A road map of what's to come (optional)

- No "funnel" structure or "panoramic" statements

4.3   Body Paragraphs

I still remember the exact moment when I first understood, with a sudden clarity, the purpose of a paragraph. I didn't have the vocabulary to say "paragraph," but I realized that a paragraph was a fence that held words. The words inside a paragraph worked together for a common purpose. They had some specific reason for being inside the same fence. This knowledge delighted me. I began to think of everything in terms of paragraphs. Our reservation was a small paragraph within the United States. My family's house was a paragraph, distinct from the other paragraphs of the LeBrets to the north, the Fords to our south and the Tribal School to the west. Inside our house, each family member existed as a separate paragraph but still had genetics and common experiences to link us. Now, using this logic, I can see my changed family as an essay of seven paragraphs: mother, father, older brother, the deceased sister, my younger twin sisters and our adopted little brother.

Sherman Alexie, "Superman and Me"

Teachers and professors assign essays not to assess how much their students know, but to assess how well they think. The way you write your body paragraphs will make the difference between simply attesting that you fulfilled yet another academic task and the more successful strategy of demonstrating your excellent analytical skills. Each body paragraph, therefore, should be designed to show off your mastery of the topic, and to delight the reader with your insights.

Here is a rough diagram of how a typical student essay might be constructed. The connecting lines represent logical connections that should be made:

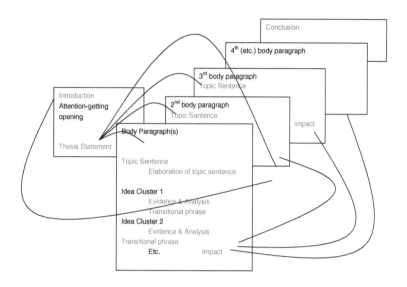

Topic Sentences

Every paragraph doesn't have to start with a topic sentence, but until you have a confident command of your writing, it can't hurt to include one, and it might as well be the first or second sentence in the paragraph. A topic sentence is like a thesis for the paragraph. It governs the content of the paragraph, stating outright what the paragraph concerns or proves and why it's relevant to your thesis. It can also provide a transitional link from the previous paragraph. Like the essay thesis, topic sentences convey a particular attitude or stance—how you feel about it. Like a thesis, the topic sentence should stand on its own to make a particular point. In fact, if you highlight your thesis and all of your topic sentences, they should constitute a complete and easily understandable outline of the essay itself—with no key concept left out. A good topic sentence is precise, not vague; interpretive, not non-committal.

Example topic sentences:

- Charlotte Perkins Gilman imagined aspects of a utopian, gender-fair society and then sought to inhabit that world.

- Plato recognized that education is key to good citizenship, and he starts, logically, with the education of the guardians.

- Establishing a strong infrastructure to support food production is also key to providing food security in Sub-Saharan Africa.

- In *Walden,* Thoreau also objects to the encroachment of material progress, as symbolized by the train that noisily transgresses the peaceful and restorative tranquility of the forest.

- The benefits of complex suture might have aided the animal in life, but would not necessarily have led had an overall impact on species longevity.

- *Not only* does William Apess allude to shared Biblical values to expose hypocrisy, *he also* leads his audience to draw their own conclusions through his use of rhetorical questions. (notice how the italicized portions provide a frame for transition)

Summing Up

A topic sentence is like a mini-thesis for the paragraph, establishing the content as well as the writer's stance on it. It's usually the first sentence in the body paragraph. Each topic sentence connects the material in that paragraph to the essay thesis.

A good topic sentence:

- Defines what this paragraph proves or considers

- Shows why it's relevant (how it supports the thesis)

- Expresses a particular stance

- Can also serve as a transition

Body Paragraphs

To build the rest of the body paragraph, arrange your evidence in logical order, and connect it with analysis that explains what the evidence means in relation to the thesis and topic sentence. Basically, a body paragraph is a trail of the inductive and deductive reasoning you derived when you analyzed the topic. This holds true regardless of what type of essay you are writing, whether the evidence is from a work of literature or art, from research sources, from personal experience, or from empirical observations. Be sure to anchor your interpretations in the actual words of the source. An even distribution of quoted evidence from the source will prevent your paragraph from sailing off to unsupportable claims and irrelevant observations or circling around the same idea over and over. Also, look back at your topic sentence from time to time to make sure that you have not drifted out of the confines of its stated territory for this paragraph.

As you move through the paragraph, do not simply drop in the evidence, but incorporate it into your own sentences. This may require trimming the lines down to the most important phrase, as these examples demonstrate:

- He describes how the soldiers "[use] a hard vocabulary to contain the terrible softness" (O'Brien, 20).

- The blow that ends Gatsby's "presumptuous little flirtation" with Daisy precedes not only the tangible crash of the day, a car accident, but also the ultimate ruin of his hope (Fitzgerald, 135).

The brackets in the first example indicate a word replaced or added. Brackets can also indicate change in tense (played to play[s]).

Notice how the first sentence is dominated by the quotation and that the lead-in to it is bland and non-committal. It's not that the quotation can't fill up most of the sentence, but that it has to serve the goal of the sentence (and the essay). In the second, an important and pithy phrase is not the center of the sentence's attention, but adds its heft to a larger point being made. It is necessary and it is convincing, but artfully subordinated to a larger idea. Notice, too, that the second example is just a claim—it still needs to be proven with further evidence and analysis.

Here is another example:

> Gatsby is labeled as a "bootlegger," a "common swindler," and "one of that bunch that hangs around Meyer Wolfsheim" (133).

Rather than taking over the sentence, this stack of evidence supports a point that will be made next, as the writer analyzes what these terms imply. The essay continues with:

> With a few subtle indictments, Tom strikes at Gatsby's most precious possession—his reputation—and initiates the collapse of his carefully constructed disguise. Furthermore, this exposure, presenting a Gatsby antithetical to his "Platonic conception of himself," begins his psychological demise as well (Fitzgerald, 98).

This is a good example of what analysis should do. This writer unpacks the evidence, explains how it works within the text or topic, moving beyond the obvious (that calling someone a bootlegger is an insult) to interpret the impact of Tom's accusations on the meaning of the novel as a whole. Good analysis supports the thesis and does not deviate from its concerns, but rather digs into the material in enough detail to make convincing connections that could only be hinted at in the essay's introduction.

In the body paragraph, strike a balance between quoted or paraphrased evidence (duly cited, in both cases) and your own explanation, connecting it to the topic sentence and thesis. You can think of the evidence as chocolate chips in a cookie—you need plenty of them, and, ideally, they should be evenly distributed. If you have three or more sentences without evidence, you may have drifted off topic, lapsed into repetition, or merely summarized the plot. If necessary, go back and anchor your statements with evidence.

For a research essay, you may quote longer lines and passages, even whole paragraphs at times. But note that for most science essays, you are not expected to quote at all, but rather to put the material into your own words, citing the author(s) at the end. This demonstrates that you have understood the concepts. For history and other social studies essays, always quote primary sources but mostly paraphrase or summarize secondary sources, except for key phrases and terms coined by the author. However, if the social studies essay is about theory, then you would quote the theorists directly where needed. In any event, when quoting, pick the pithiest, most pertinent, most compelling piece of evidence to quote. Weave in the evidence with your own ideas. In research essays the necessity to demarcate your ideas from those you gleaned from your sources is crucial, else you may be accused of plagiarism. Always identify your sources, either by including the author's name and the date and title of the work in the sentence or by citing it at the end. See Chapter 7 on Documenting Sources for details on how to do this for various disciplines.

As the essay moves from one piece of evidence or idea cluster to the next, include transitional words and phrases to serve as guideposts to the reader. In effect, transitions announce that one idea chunk has finished and a new one is being presented. And here again, just as the thesis and topic sentences provide a skeleton of the essay, the topic sentence and idea chunks provide a skeleton of the body paragraph.

You can think of a body paragraph as consisting of:

```
Body Paragraph(s)

Topic Sentence

        Elaboration of topic sentence

Idea  Cluster 1

      Evidence & Analysis

      Transitional phrase

Idea Cluster 2

      Evidence & Analysis

      Transitional phrase

      Etc.

Impact
```

Transitions provide continuity as well as dramatize the contrasts between ideas, to indicate that rather than circling around the same ideas, that the paragraph is going somewhere.

Examples of transitional words and phrases:

Although	Hence
And yet	However
As a result	In addition
Because	In consequence
By contrast	In fact
Consequently	It is clear that
Considering	The fact that
Despite	Nevertheless
Due to	Next
Equally significant	Since
For example	Then
For this reason	Therefore
Furthermore	Thus

Further cohesion lies in strategically repeating key words and phrases throughout the paragraph and essay. These words representing important thematic strings can be varied slightly to avoid sounding repetitious. As you write you may inadvertently include ideas that do not fit into the topic of the paragraph. During the editing process you will clean up the thematic strings, deleting inappropriate ones or moving them into another paragraph where they fit better. This is where your pre-planning pays off, for having identified the core words and phrases up front, you can foreground them deliberately.

Sample body paragraph for a literature essay:

> The transformative power of the Vietnam War is further exemplified in Mary Anne's story. An innocent girl in a pink sweater and culottes, she becomes first curious about and then fascinated with the power of killing, finally joining the Greenies in their night raids. Upon her return, Fossie realizes he has lost her when he notices that "There was no emotion in her stare, no sense of a person behind it. But the grotesque part… was her jewelry. At the girl's throat was a necklace of human tongues" (110). The necklace, clearly a trophy commemorating many enemy killings, stands as an outer marker of her inner transformation—into a complete savage. The fact that the tips of the tongues are "curled upward as if caught in a final shrill syllable" can be read either as a scream of fear or possibly a shrill of triumph, for the necklace celebrates death and killing (111). It is clear that the primal savage that lies deep within every civilized human has surfaced and taken over Mary Anne's personality. Her human warmth and compassion have disappeared, leaving her eyes "utterly flat and indifferent" and unresponsive to Mark's entreaties (110). Mark sees no person behind her stare because everything she used to be has been stripped away by the war; only her pink sweater and culottes attest to her former innocence. Mary Anne's story demonstrates that the Vietnam War experience is not just devastating, but dehumanizing. It taps into a side of humanity that should not be released.

Here is another example, this time on a historical account:

> Gertrude Morgan, in her captivity narrative, rationalizes westward expansion by vilifying the Indians and by creating an appealing picture of the West. The Gold Rush drew hordes of settlers to the West; Morgan captures the allure of the region by describing its

natural beauty in terms of gold and gems. Her words, charged with significance, reflect the hopeful expectations held by her readers regarding the west, a land of wealth and opportunity, beauty and grandeur. The grasses of the plain are "gilded" with the sun's rays and resemble "moulten gold and emeralds" (Morgan 395). A "melancholy, bluish mist" lends a dream-like quality to the "boundless" prairie (395). The choice of wording imbues the land with treasure waiting to be discovered. And, according to Morgan, the dreams of her readers are not far from reality. Her husband started "an extensive and lucrative business in Sacramento," proving true the "dazzling accounts of newspapers" at the time (396, 395).The premise of success having motivated the westward expansion, the characterization of the Indians as savages justified it. As the white men of Morgan's expedition "stood nobly," the Indians who attacked them "came dashing down with deafening yells and whoops" (398). She clearly indicates that honorable whites like her would make better settlers than the ignorant brutes they encountered, thus rationalizing the takeover of Indian land.

This is from a science essay:

New techniques in general farm management can also play a large role in food security for Africa. Initially, farmers need to be taught simple techniques such as using fertilizer, rotating crops, and planting in rows. In places where this has been done, it has taken only two years for farmers to produce a surplus (Beard 1997). At the same time, new technologies that enable precision fertilizer application can also increase efficiency. In the United States, farmers are using GPS systems to avoid wasteful overlapping when applying fertilizer by tractor, as well as new software that tracks yields by crop location, allowing farmers to target specific areas for more or less amounts of fertilizer (Little 2009). With fertilizer prices rising, efficiency is paramount. Since fertilizer can double yields, farmers who use it efficiently can produce significant surpluses, thus making it possible to invest in more fertilizer and more diverse crops, with compounding benefits.

Notice that in each sample body paragraph, the topic sentence introduces a significant topic in a clear and direct manner. The paragraph is coherent—it makes sense and stays on topic. Where used, quoted evidence is blended into the author's own sentences and followed by one or more sentences that analyze, discussing the effect of the quoted words. Notice also that the citation goes at the end of the sentence, followed by a period. In the science paragraph, sources are not quoted, but paraphrased, but again, a citation appears at the end of the sentence. Whenever you paraphrase, be sure to preserve the sense and intent of the original wording.

Summing Up

Body paragraphs do the main work of the essay by presenting evidence and analysis that supports the thesis. They are structured like a mini-essay, with a topic sentence that is like a thesis statement that will be proven with evidence and explanation in the paragraph.

A tidy structure in the body paragraphs of an essay demonstrates the writer's care and logical approach, and includes a topic sentence, carefully selected and concise evidence woven into the writer's own sentences, and analysis that ties the evidence to the thesis while developing ideas in depth. Transitional words provide a road map for the reader.

Elements of body paragraphs:

- The topic sentence stating the point of the paragraph, and its elaboration, if needed

- The evidence, incorporated into your own sentences and evenly distributed throughout the paragraph

- The development of your argument through analysis explaining how the evidence proves your point

- Impact statement explaining why the idea is important

- Transitions between idea "chunks" and connecting this paragraph to the previous or following one

4.4 Conclusions

One of the least interesting approaches to concluding an essay is one of the most frequently taught: to summarize the main points of the essay, the points the reader has just finished reading. How boring! While repeating main ideas is of value in a speech, in an essay it leaves the reader with the impression that the writer has lost interest in her topic and is merely finishing it in a perfunctory manner. Instead, treat your reader to a flourish at the end, as a symphony composer does. Your conclusion doesn't need to solve the world's problems in two sentences, but it does need to send the reader away with the impression that what she has learned is important and applicable to her life, for example, that she has learned some insight about the world or human nature. Therefore, in concluding, raise some of the wider implications of the thesis, such as how F. Scott Fitzgerald's portrayal of the moral bankruptcy of the wealthy class during the Jazz Age has relevance to our times, or that Napoleon's optimism about his officers' skills is a reminder of the hubris or overconfidence that often blinds leaders. You can also turn a key word or phrase from the essay to good effect. For example, in an essay on materialism that refers to our "overstuffed closets" that concept could be turned to create a witty sendoff about the relative value of an "overstuffed wallet." Be careful not to overstate the case. Your essay on World War II cannot promise the key to end all wars.

Before you write your conclusion, go back to your introduction and thesis and make sure that you have delivered the essay you promised. Now is the time to tune up your introduction, perhaps adding an image or concept that you can return to in the conclusion, to give the essay a sense of coming full circle to a tidy closure. Remember that for an exam essay, the conclusion can be brief—even a sentence long. But for other essays, invest some time in crafting a conclusion that does more than summarize what you just finished saying, and what your reader just finished reading. It's your last chance to make a strong impression on your reader. Consider using a rhetorical device to formalize the message, as this student does:

> If drugs continue to be easily procured, if rehabilitation programs continue to offer no forgiveness, if society continues to treat addiction as a character flaw instead of a disease, then the world will never escape the hypnotic whirlpool of drug addiction. These factors are all equally to blame, so that criminalizing the individual drug addict is itself a social crime. To end the destructive behaviors with which society seems so enthralled, we must revise our broken approach to reducing drug use and drug addiction.

The parallel structure of the sentence (If...if...if) leads eloquently to a call to action inspiring the reader to feel a sense of responsibility about the topic. Here is an ending to an essay on reality television that aptly uses a quotation as well as a rhetorical question:

> So the next time you seek entertainment from a reality television show, consider the impact the participants antics will have on young people watching the show, and recall the words of Immanuel Kant, "Out of the crooked timber of humanity no straight thing can be made." Is this the kind of entertainment that builds character?

This student turns a phrase based on the central issue of his essay on water conservation to end with a powerful warning:

> Nothing can prevent the western United States from running out of water unless the Bureau of Reclamation can wash itself clean of the corruption and foolishness that have hampered it since its foundation. If the Bureau fails to revise its mission, the American West will be remembered only as a mirage, another desert civilization obliterated by government incompetence.

Here, a student ends his literary analysis essay with a bold flourish of insight and powerful language:

> Fitzgerald's *The Great Gatsby*, does indeed criticize American society and its lust for material wealth during the Jazz Age; yet Gatsby, the protagonist who in so many ways manifests all that is wrong with that American Dream, is held up as a noble hero. While the noble hero's quest has becomes tainted by Jazz Age society, Gatsby does not represent this decline. His desires, while seemingly superficial, are actually testaments to selfless devotion and the quest for a brighter future. Jay Gatsby exists outside of the Jazz Age, in the realm of mythopoeia, a noble hero of the America habit of dreaming great dreams.

Summing Up

Your conclusion is your last chance to impress your reader and send him off with something important to think about. Rather than restate the thesis and main points, use this opportunity to expand on the original thesis and tie it to larger implications about life, literature, society, and so on. Your conclusion might return to a detail in the introduction, with greater understanding, or develop further a central, key term. It should be written with boldness and a flair, because this is your last chance to impress and please your reader.

A conclusion can include:

- A call to action
- The wider implications of the thesis
- A return to a detail from the introduction (framing the essay)
- A turn on a key word or phrase used in the essay
- A rhetorical flourish that gives a sense of closure

GETTING OUT THE FIRST DRAFT

If you are writing an exam essay, then you do not have the luxury of writing a first draft, but it would help you to consider it one, to hush up that inner editor who has a tendency to nag you to perfect each word as you write. Your goal in writing a draft is to write without self-judgment, knowing that you will have time later on to revise for clarity and style. But before writing, put together an outline or plan of attack first, so you have a road map to follow.

Start the draft anywhere—in the middle, or even at the end. Writing a body paragraph first will probably be easier than starting at the beginning with the introduction. Often you think of good ideas for the introduction while working on the main part of the essay. Keep your outline in front of you, so that you stay on topic. You can even write out a sentence at the top of your page that starts: This paragraph is proving that _____. As you work, try not to get stuck on finding the exact word. Put in a placeholder word or phrase, highlight it, and keep going. Your brain will probably produce a better word while it is busy with a later part of the essay, and even if it doesn't, you can revise it as you are editing the whole draft and see the shape of it coming together.

Remember to distribute evidence throughout the essay, in the chocolate-chips-in-the-cookie pattern referred to in Chapter 4, or to paraphrase it, as is expected for science and secondary sources for social studies essays. Be vigilant about citing sources as you go, even if only in abbreviated form, putting all cited material into quotation marks. You don't want inadvertently to present the words of others as your own. As you proceed, some of the evidence will not fit the way you expected it to. While you can modify the verb tense or pronouns to fit your sentence, do not distort the point of your paragraph just to include something that is really irrelevant to your point, no matter how interesting it is. Some items will fall to the cutting room floor as you write. Likewise, you may discover that you need additional information. Make a note of it, and keep on writing.

A draft is not like free writing. In free-writing, you can follow anywhere your ideas lead you. In a draft, you are constructing meaning, so be scrupulous about what to include and omit. Make sure the evidence really does support your claims, and if any of it fails to do so, either change the point of the paragraph or search for better evidence. Sometimes it is in the draft stage that you realize that your thesis does not hold true. If this happens, do not panic! Hopefully, you started early enough ahead that you have time to step back, perhaps do some more reading, and revise your thesis to fit the facts, to produce a stronger essay.

Even with a precise and detailed outline, some of the paragraphs may go astray, some may need to be subdivided, some may require additional thought and further investigation. To keep your momentum going, you can flag the places that need shoring up and come back to them later. Take advantage of a full-steam-ahead productiveness as long as you can keep it going, checking your outline from time to time to make sure you are on track.

Ideally, put a day or two between your first draft and revising it. It helps to clear your mind so that you tackle revision when you are fresh and creatively ready.

Example Draft Body Paragraph:

> The United States had an imperialistic relationship with Cuba [when did it start?]. By 1959, "the United States accounted for 74 percent of Cuban export sales and supplied 65 percent of its imports" (Dominguez 149). Cuba was a huge source of agricultural imports of the United States. It also had built infrastructure in Cuba so that it could do business there, railroads to move goods and telephones for taking orders, and electricity which was not pervasive in Cuba. "In addition, American interests dominated many key activities, including telephone and electric light and power companies, which operated in an atmosphere of general public hostility. A major railroad system serving the eastern half of the island was American-controlled" (Bonsal 265). This infrastructure made

other businesses take root in Cuba, owned by Cubans. This potential lay in the very success of U.S. enterprise, which actually resulted in making opportunities for Cuban entrepreneurs. Those Cubans who worked for Americans saved their wages and built up personal capital in order to start their own businesses. [What businesses did Cubans own?] The impact of U.S. involvement had more than just a profitable effect on the U.S.; it also sparked important growth in the Cuban middle class.

Notice that the writer has highlighted words he wants to revise, and has included a reminder to himself to do some further research.

Summing Up

Prepare a full outline, and then begin writing anywhere that appeals to you. Write quickly, keeping your inner editor at bay. Simply highlight phrases and words that you want to upgrade later. Try to put the correct actor into the subject of sentences where you can, although you can modify to remove passive voice during the editing phase. Use plenty of evidence, cutting it down to the pithy parts and incorporating it into your own sentences. Make the evidence flow by using ellipses and bracketed changes where necessary.

A draft includes:

- Well distributed evidence

- Citations and quotation marks for all quoted material

- Placeholder words for later revision

- Fully developed paragraphs

- Flags for further research and missing items

6

REVISING

The most difficult aspect of revision is making the shift from the role of the writer to the role of the editor. One way to arrive at this helpful distance is to allow a few days to pass between finishing the first draft and reading it again to make improvements. When you sit down to edit, try to approach the reading from the vantage point of having to convince someone who is not quite in agreement with your thesis and who may not connect the dots from one idea to the next. The suggested method that follows is based on revising a persuasive essay draft, but you can apply the ideas here to the revision of any kind of essay.

Allow plenty of time to revise. Most professional writers spend more time revising than they do writing the original draft. The more you balance your time as a professional would, the more professional your writing will become. There are four main areas of editing, each calling for a slightly different kind of attention. If you have time, make four passes through your draft, attending to each area in turn.

Structure

Take a bird's-eye view of the essay and look at its overall structure, without considering the content in detail just yet. Starting with the title, ask yourself if it clearly indicates the topic to be discussed, in an intriguing way. Now read just the thesis statement and each of the topic sentences in your body paragraphs, skipping over the rest. Is the thesis statement arguable and important? More critically—do the topic sentences address the right aspects of the thesis and prove it correct? Are all of the topic sentences at the right level of detail, and do they, together with the thesis, comprise a logical flow of ideas? In their literary essays, some students make the mistake of treating evidence as the topic of body paragraphs. For example, it is not uncommon for novice writers to organize an essay about a novel in which each body paragraph is about a different character. While it is not necessarily wrong to organize an essay by character, a weak essay will have topic sentences that simply announce the character to be discussed, instead of making a strong link to the thesis in the topic sentence. Notice the difference between:

Weak: Another example of the American Dream gone awry was Wilson, the mechanic who was married to Myrtle.

Better: The American Dream can also go awry for members of the lower class who are dangerously dependent on the corrupt elite, as illustrated by the character George Wilson, a garage mechanic.

The second version announces the idea that the body paragraph will prove, while the first one merely announces who is going to serve as an example, giving the reader no indication of the idea to be developed.

Notice the difference between the thesis statement and topic sentences from two different essays:

Weak

Thesis:	Though branded as a sinner, Hester Prynne's standard of morality is actually much higher than that of her community.
Topic sentence 1:	Hester married Roger Chillingworth when she was a young girl and she soon regretted her decision.
Topic sentence 2:	Hester provides her artistic gift even as the entire community chastises her.
Topic sentence 3:	An important and timeless moral lesson is that of truth.
Conclusion topic sentence:	This lesson in life is that one must "Be true" to oneself.

Strong

Thesis:	In *The Scarlet Letter*, Hawthorne proves the irony that sometimes when humans attempt to punish others, they actually exalt them for their sins.
Topic sentence 1:	After her public chastisement, Hester Prynne becomes a "living sermon" in which her very existence has changed from signifying an example of sin to a reminder of divine compassion (Hawthorne 44).
Topic sentence 2:	Not only does the public glorify sin, sinners themselves sometimes fetishize their own sin as if it were a holy relic.
Topic sentence 3:	The dual nature of sin is most obvious in the scaffold in the center of town.
Topic sentence 4:	Hawthorne draws clear parallels between Hester standing alone on the scaffold and Jesus nailed alone on his crucifix.
Conclusion topic sentence:	In exposing the irony at the heart of social punishment, Hawthorne levies criticism as society in general, in unambiguous terms, unlike many of the other messages he sends in this novel.

Notice how in the weak example, the first topic sentence, while not a complete digression, does not clearly link to it. Topic sentences should be quite obvious and direct. A better topic sentence would be, "Hester's sin can be justified by the circumstances of her marriage." The second topic sentence actually addresses the thesis appropriately, but the third and the concluding paragraph topics sentence do not seem to relate at all, though the content of the paragraph might actually do so. When topic sentences are unclear, the reader loses the thread of the argument and become frustrated with the essay. In the strong example, each of the topic sentences clearly addresses a pertinent, unique, and interesting proof of the thesis; in addition, they present a logical progression from the community reaction, to the personal impact, to the nature of sin itself.

After reviewing the skeleton of your essay, check the works cited or bibliography to make sure that it is complete.

Structure Checklist:

- Is the thesis arguable and important?
- Do the topic sentences prove thesis and flow logically?
- Is the bibliography complete?

Development of Ideas

Now that you have checked the overall structure, you need to address the most important aspect of revision—reviewing the substance of the essay. To do so, you will read each paragraph as an independent unit, checking whether it is serves its unique purpose. Don't be afraid to revise heavily, even to replace much or all of a whole paragraph. Your work here will improve the essay you are writing, but, more importantly, it will help you write more efficiently next time.

Starting with the introduction, ask yourself if it still relevant to the essay. Many times writers "write their way" to a new understanding of the material, making their own introduction obsolete. Tune it up as needed. Also get rid of any bloated phrasing, trimming the introduction to the core ideas that support to the thesis. As a general rule, the introduction should be less than half as long as the body paragraphs. Tidy up the wording of the thesis statement, so that it vividly states the argument your essay will prove. Add some zest to the opening line, too, to grab the reader's attention and establish a strong ethos.

Now read each body paragraph carefully. The first order of business is to determine that each one supports the thesis with significant ideas. Ask yourself if you have developed the ideas thoroughly enough, so that all important insights and implications have been explained. Mark oversimplifications and take the time to brainstorm your way to more depth. Consider whether all the ideas in the paragraph really belong together, whether some ideas need to be separated, some paragraphs merged. You can improve the expression of the ideas as you go, or get them down in draft form and revise to improve the language in a separate pass.

Also check the distribution of evidence, perhaps even highlighting it. Notice how the sample below has a fairly even distribution of evidence, indicating that the ideas are well anchored.

> The gray-cloaked townspeople represent the harsh Puritan mindset and the societal restrictions that disapprove of and punish sin. The austere mentality of the Puritans prevents them from accepting Hester, even after she has worked to redeem herself. For the pious Puritans, "religion and law [are] almost identical" (Hawthorne 56); Hester's crime not only breaks the law, but also places her soul in jeopardy and threatens the Puritan theocracy. The matrons of the town fear that other young ladies will begin to defy the law as well, so they criticize the magristrates for being "merciful overmuch," proclaiming that "this woman has brought shame upon us all, and ought to die" (36). However, the Puritans view the scarlet letter through a fog of harsh morality. They see Hester holding a child born of adultery, but they do not know of Hester and Dimmesdale's passion or of Chillingworth's crime against Hester's youth. They only see a violation of law and the necessity to bring Hester into line through humiliation. Nina Baym in "Passion and Authority in The Scarlet Letter" notes that in this era, to "forget the claims of society is to sin against it" (Baym 209). However, Hester's crime is a sin only because her society deems it to be. The pressure of Puritan society turns Hester's act of love into an instance of ignominy.

In the example above, the quotations are integrated into the writer's own sentences. Verify that your quotations support your claims and trim them as necessary to flow naturally with your own ideas. Also scrutinize the citations to make sure that quoted and paraphrased material is properly attributed and accurately represented. Now is the time to double-check the works cited list to make sure that there is an entry for each source, too.

Look for digressions and evidence that is not relevant to purpose of the paragraph. Do the ideas proceed logically? Or is there is a jump from one idea to the next? If so, add the necessary sentences to connect them. If you have lapsed into plot summary, replace it with your own analysis. Next consider whether the paragraph does its job. You might write out the purpose of the paragraph before reading it, then decide whether it has met its goal. If necessary, add more explanation and evidence.

Development of Ideas Checklist:

- Is the introduction lean and focused?

- Is the evidence well distributed?

- Do ideas flow, without mere plot summary or digressions?

- Are explanations thorough, yet concise?

- Does each paragraph achieve its purpose?

- Does the conclusion expand on the thesis?

Language

Refer to Chapter 8: Developing Style for specific suggestions about improving the phrasing of the essay. Then read the essay aloud, listening for awkward wording or language that obscures your meaning. Replace any weak verbs (to be, etc.) with strong ones. Remove pretentious or overly flowery language that sounded lofty when you wrote it but that rings falsely now that you are reading it in a different mode. Replace it with clear, direct language that is grammatically correct and precise. Some students have an addiction to the thesaurus key on their computers, which obscures their writing with words whose meaning or connotation does not quite fit and thus may skew the sentence just enough to throw the reader off. While you don't want to shy away from using advanced vocabulary, you do want to make sure that each word fits the ideas precisely. Notice the difference between the original draft version of this sentence and the edited version:

Original:

> While some seek a pathway to transcend the reliance on the coping mechanism for vehement conflict, others are subject to the intoxicating power that it provides and fall yet further into its brutal graces.

It's fairly obvious that the thesaurus key contributed to the clumsiness of the sentence above! Here is the edited version:

> While most people avoid violence, others become strangely attracted to it.

Here is a draft body paragraph that contains good ideas, but they are obscured by clumsy language:

> As the novella progresses, Conrad creates an icon with which the reader may associate the Wilderness: Kurtz's hut in the heart of the African jungle. Creating perhaps the most frightfully savage image of the novella, Marlow describes a circle of human heads, mounted on poles, surrounding the dwelling (55). Marlow also notices "a narrow white line of ... teeth ... smiling" upon the "shrunken" and "dry" faces (55), as if those decapitated were happy to see their former heads constitute part of a ritualistic monument to the Lord of the Wilderness. As the image of Kurtz comes to its surprisingly mortal end – explicitly conceived by Conrad to ensure that light triumphs over dark; good over evil; Europe over the heathens of Africa – Marlow's narration is uncharacteristically succinct: "[Kurtz] cried in a whisper at some image, at some vision – he cried out twice, a cry that was no more than a breath – 'The horror! The horror!'" (67). However, despite the surprising brevity, Kurtz's final words elucidate his place in the text; he recognizes – in his final, dying breath – that he has become part of the "horror" of the Wilderness.

While not without merit, this paragraph is hard to follow. Some of the sentences are "backwards" in that the actor does not appear in the subject. Many of the quotations distract the reader rather than support the ideas in the paragraph, and do not flow smoothly within the writer's own sentences. Finally, there are many words that do not fit, confusing the reader. Several sentences need to be reworked, a few quotations trimmed, and some vocabulary replaced.

Here it is revised for clarity:

> Kurtz's adopted home is the locus and symbol of the "utter savagery" of the African jungle (12). In perhaps the most frightful of many savage images in the novella, Marlow describes a circle of human heads, mounted on poles, surrounding the dwelling, with "a narrow white line of ... teeth ... smiling" upon the "shrunken" and "dry" faces (55), as if the decapitated were happy to see their former heads form a ritualistic monument to the Lord of the Wilderness. As Kurtz comes to his surprising mortal end, Marlow's narration is uncharacteristically succinct: "[Kurtz] cried

out twice, a cry that was no more than a breath—'The horror!
The horror!'" (67). These final words reveal the ultimate
purpose of Kurtz in the text, for they convey that Kurtz has
himself become part of the "horror" of the African Wilderness,
and now tragically realizes this. Thus the traditional novelistic
ending that Conrad on one hand supplies—a death in which light
triumphs over dark, good over evil, Europe over the heathens of
Africa—he also undercuts, for Kurtz emblemizes the descent into
moral iniquity that colonialism always entails.

The revised version puts the main ideas onto center stage by removing
some of the confusingly complex diction. The ideas are complex
enough—the aim it to express them simply.

Language Checklist:

- Is the major actor the subject of sentences?

- Are the verbs strong?

- Is the phrasing concise, yet clear?

- Are quotations trimmed to fit and flow?

- Is the vocabulary precise?

Mechanics

In the final editing pass, check for mechanical errors in punctuation,
citations, comma usage, and title punctuation. Remember that
longer works should be in *italics*, shorter ones in "quotation marks."
If you tend to have problems with comma placement, as so many
students do, look up the rules of comma usage (in general, commas
separate; semi-colons join) and scrutinize each comma in the essay.
Also remember that commas and periods generally go inside of the
quotation marks for cited material, except when a parenthetical
citation follows it:

>   **Incorrect:**   When Tom begins to feel "hot whips of panic",
>   he becomes cognizant that both Daisy and Myrtle,
>   who were recently so "secure and inviolate", were
>   "slipping precipitately from his control." (125)

Correct: When Tom begins to feel "hot whips of panic,"
                    he becomes cognizant that both Daisy and Myrtle,
                    who were recently so "secure and inviolate," were
                    "slipping precipitately from his control" (125).

Finally, look over your works cited or bibliography to correct any punctuation or formatting errors in it. Use a recent guide to the citation style you are using (MLA, APA, CMS, etc.) and scrutinize each entry. It is always impressive to present a thorough and mechanically accurate bibliography, and it avoids misrepresenting your sources.

Mechanics Checklist:

- Is the title punctuated correctly?

- Are commas and semi-colons correctly used?

- Are punctuation marks correctly placed in quoted materials?

- Is the works cited or bibliography correctly presented?

7

DOCUMENTING SOURCES

7.1 When and How to Cite Sources

Notice that the title of this chapter does not include *whether* to document sources! The purpose of documenting sources is to acknowledge the origination of the works that support your essay as well as research suggestions for your reader to explore. Check with your instructor about which standard of source citation to use, the most common being MLA (Modern Language Association), APA (American Psychological Association), CMS (Chicago Manual of Style), and CSE (Council of Science Editors). Generally, use MLA or CMS for humanities essays, APA for social studies essays, and CSE for science essays. You will find detailed guidelines for each of these online, but this chapter provides an overall guideline as well as examples of the most frequently cited sources: books, articles, and web pages. But first, this introduction addresses when you must cite sources and how to avoid plagiarizing.

Staying organized is crucial to success. If you are meticulous in note-taking during research, citing sources within your essay and listing the texts in your works cited or bibliography will be relatively easy. A top priority is to differentiate between your own words and those from your sources in your notes. Put all direct quotations into quotation marks ("*x*") and cite the page number at the end of the last quoted sentence. As you take notes **include the author name and title on every quoted passage**. This may seem redundant but it prevents getting confused about the correct source when you cut and paste evidence into your essay. Put all of your own comments inside [brackets] or use some other means to distinguish them from quoted material. Stay true to the text—make sure that you represent responsibly what the source says. If you need to omit words, use **ellipses** to indicate this, but do not remove words when that will shift the meaning of the passage. Your cited material must represent the source consistently and accurately, even when you paraphrase.

Common knowledge does not have to be cited at all. Facts, dates, and standard, accepted knowledge (such as that a given writer is from the Romantic Period or that many Sub-Saharan African nations struggle with AIDS infection) do not need to be cited. These do not need citations because they do not represent someone's original idea or research. One accepted standard for common knowledge is that if the information appears in three or more sources, without citation, then it need not be cited. Beyond these guidelines, when in doubt, cite it.

You do have to cite:

- Direct quotations

- Paraphrased ideas (even if you change every word)

- Unique ideas

To see how to properly quote and paraphrase material taken from a text, let's start with this short passage, a definition of philosophy, written by Bertrand Russell[1]:

> Philosophy, as I shall understand the word, is something intermediate between theology and science. Like theology, it consists of speculations on matters as to which definite knowledge has, so far, been unascertainable; but like science, it appeals to human reason rather than to authority, whether that of tradition or that of revelation. All definite knowledge—so I should contend—belongs to science; all dogma as to what surpasses definite knowledge belongs to theology. But between theology and science there is a No Man's Land, exposed to attack from both sides; this No Man's Land is philosophy. Almost all the questions of most interest to speculative minds are such as science cannot answer, and the confident answers of theologians no longer seem so convincing as they did in former centuries. (Russell xiii)

---

1 From the introduction to Russell's *A History of Western Philosophy and Its Connection with Political and Social Circumstances from the Earliest Times to the Present Day,* George Allen and Unwin Ltd., London, 1962, p. xiii.

To use Russell's actual words, put them into quotation marks:

> According to philosopher Bertrand Russell, philosophy is "intermediate between theology and science" and addresses questions that "science cannot answer, and the confident answers of theologians no longer seem so convincing as they did in former centuries" (Russell xiii).

It would not be legitimate to change a word here and there and not cite your source. This is plagiarizing:

> Philosophy exists in the No Man's Land between science and theology, answering questions that science cannot answer and that theology answers, but does so without convincing.

So is this:

> Philosophy exists in the "No Man's Land" between science and theology, answering questions that science cannot answer and that theology answers, but does so without convincing (Russell xiii).

In the above example, all of the ideas come from Russell, but it seems that just the quoted phrase is attributed to him. In other words, don't mix paraphrasing and quoting in the same sentence. And be careful not to let new ideas creep into the paraphrase. Preserve the exact sense of the original, but express it in your own words.

You can cite Russell through paraphrasing, as long as you attribute the material to him. The sentence below is not plagiarism, because the citation indicates that all of the ideas in the sentence come from Russell, which is true:

> Philosophy exists between science and theology, answering questions that science does not answer and that theology answers, but does so without convincing (Russell xiii).

You can also put the author's name into the text and thus cite only the page number:

> Russell explains that Philosophy exists between science and theology, answering questions that science cannot answer and that theology answers, but does so without convincing (xiii).

To indicate a break between Russell's ideas and your own, move the citation:

> Philosophy exists between science and theology, answering questions that science cannot answer and that theology answers, but does so without convincing (Russell xiii), and it has become even more respected than either of those disciplines.

To cull out words you do not want, use ellipses (...) to indicate where words have been removed:

> "All definite knowledge...belongs to science; all dogma as to what surpasses definite knowledge belongs to theology" (Russell xiii).

You can also change the verb tense to fit the quotation into your own sentence more fluently, using brackets to indicate the change:

> Russell explains that philosophy came about when there were "the questions...that science c[ould] not answer, and the confident answers of theologians no longer seem[ed] so convincing as they [had] in former centuries.

Finally, if you decide to paraphrase several sentences, you do not have to repeat the citation in each sentence; instead, mention the author's name at the beginning and write the paraphrase in such a way as to indicate that these ideas belong to the source, not to you:

> Russell examines the defining differences between philosophy and science. He suggests that science involves knowledge, while theology deals in dogma and that we look to theology when science cannot answer our questions.

Of course, if you are using a citation system that includes the year, all of the above would have the year following the author's name. For example:

> Russell (2010) examines the defining differences between philosophy and science...

Summing Up

To avoid plagiarism, carefully keep track of what material comes straight from sources, what has been paraphrased, and what are your own words. Then, cite each instance of quoted or paraphrased material responsibly, putting quoted material into quotation marks and following quoted and paraphrased material with the name and page of the source where it came from. Any source you consult and take information from must be cited!

Documenting sources responsibly includes:

- Finding reliable primary and secondary sources

- Recording source information during note-taking

- Making sure to distinguish between source words and yours

- Responsibly paraphrasing

- Trimming quotations to fit essay sentences

- Putting all quoted material into quotation marks

The guidelines that follow offer a representative sample of the most frequently used source types and how to cite them. There are dozens more types of sources, from government documents, to blogs, to dissertations. You can find detailed instructions for any type of source by searching the internet for the most recent guidelines (the Purdue University Online Writing Lab website is one excellent resource), or you can use one of the many online citation generators (www.citationcenter.net and www.bibme.org are free, accurate, and ad-free). Note that since 2009, MLA and APA no longer require URLs for web pages.

Citation Systems by Discipline

Here are the major disciplines and the citation system they tend to use. Many disciplines use more than one style. In the sciences, there are confusing variations within a given style as well. So check with your instructor before deciding which citation system to use:

Anthropology	CMS (Chicago Manual of Style)
Architecture	APA (American Psychological Association)

Arts	MLA (Modern Language Association)
Biology	CBE (Council of Biology Editors)
Business	APA (American Psychological Association)
Chemistry	ACS (American Chemical Society)
Education	APA (American Psychological Association)
English/Humanities	MLA (Modern Language Association) or CMS (Chicago Manual of Style)
Engineering	IEEE (Institute of Electrical and Electronics Engineers)
Earth Science	CSE (Council of Science Editors) or GSA (Geological Society of America)
Environmental Science	CSE (Council of Science Editors)
Geology	CSE (Council of Science Editors) or GSA (Geological Society of America)
History	CMS (Chicago Manual of Style) or Turabian
Information Systems	CMS (Chicago Manual of Style)
Journalism	Associated Press Stylebook
Law	The Bluebook System
Linguistics	APA (American Psychological Association)
Mathematics	AMA (American Mathematical Society)
Management	AMA (American Management Association)
Medicine	AMA (American Medical Association)
Nursing	APA (American Psychological Association)
Philosophy	MLA (Modern Language Association) or CMS (Chicago Manual of Style)
Physics	AIP (American Institute of Physics)
Psychology	APA (American Psychological Association)
Political Science	APSA (American Political Science Association)
Social Science	APA (American Psychological Association) or CMS (Chicago Manual of Style)
Sociology	ASA (American Sociological Association)

7.2   Formatting Citations

MLA (Modern Language Association)

MLA style source documentation is used in most humanities subjects. In MLA documentation, source material is followed immediately in the text by uses parenthetical citations (author name pg #). A Works Cited page is provided at the end of the essay. This guide follows the MLA format updated in 2009.

When citing a source in your essay, put the author name and page in parentheses after you quote or paraphrase a source. If you have used the author name(s) within your sentence, include only the page number in parentheses. If you are using more than one work by a given author, distinguish them by supplying the title (or at least the first part of it). For sources without an author name, simply include the title and page number. MLA does not utilize footnotes, and actually discourages their use. You would only supply a footnote to suggest further reading on a topic you discuss.

When formatting your Works Cited page, skip to a new page, and arrange the works alphabetically (ignoring "A, "An," and "The" in the beginning of the title). Use *italics*, not underlining, for titles of longer works. Double space the titles and use a hanging indent for titles that exceed one line. MLA encourages efficient numbering (250–55, not 250–255). Also include for each entry, the medium (film, print, web, DVD, etc.). Do not include URLs.

Sample Works Cited entries

Book

> Lastname, Firstname. *Title of Book*. Place of Publication: Publisher, Year of Publication. Medium of Publication.

> Friedman, Thomas L. *Hot, Flat and Crowded: Why We Need a Green Revolution—and How It Can Renew America*. New York, NY: Farrar, Straus and Giroux, 2008. Print.

Article in a Book

> Lastname, First name. "Title of Essay." *Title of Collection*. Ed. Editor's Name(s). Place of Publication: Publisher, Year. Page range of entry. Medium of Publication.

Wurdemann, John G. F. "A Physician's Notes on Cuba." *The Cuba Reader: History, Culture, Politics*. Eds. Aviva Chomsky, Barry Carr, Pamela Maria Smorkaloff. Durham, NC: Duke University Press, 2004. 39–43. Print.

Magazine Article

Author(s). "Title of Article." *Title of Periodical* Day Month Year: pages. Medium of publication.

"Singing a Different Tune." *The Economist* 14–20 Nov. 2009: 73–74. Print.

Journal Article

Author(s). "Title of Article." *Title of Journal* Volume. Issue (Year): pages. Medium of publication.

Victor, David G. and Linda Yueh. "The New Energy Order: Managing Insecurities in the Twenty-first Century." *Foreign Affairs* 89.1 (2010): 61–73. Print.

Article in a Web Magazine

Author. "Title of article." *Title of Web Magazine*. Publisher name, Publication date. Medium of publication. Date of access. Use *n.p.* if no publisher name is given and *n.d.* if no publishing date is given.

Garber, Kent. "The Green Energy Economy: What It Will Take To Get There." *U.S. News & World Report*. 20 Mar. 2009. U.S. News & World Report. Web. 2 Feb. 2010.

Web Page

Editor, author, or compiler name (if available). *Name of Site*. Version number. Name of institution/organization affiliated with the site (sponsor or publisher). Day Month Year of resource creation (if available). Medium of publication. Date of access.

If there is no sponsor or publisher, use the abbreviation N.p. (no publisher). If there is no date of publication on the site, use n.d. (no date).

Narey, Wayne. "Elizabethan Worldview." *Luminarium*, 2 Aug 2006. Web. 2 Feb 2010.

Image

> Artist name. *Name of Work.* Date of creation. Repository, city where work is housed. *Website.* Medium of publication. Date accessed.

> Diebenkorn, Richard. *Berkeley No. 52.* 1955. National Gallery of Art, Washington, DC. *National Gallery of Art.* Web. 2 Feb. 2010.

Blog

> Author name. "title or subject of the posting." *Name of the blog.* Name of institution/organization affiliated with the site (sponsor or publisher). Day Month Year of post. medium of publication (Web). Day Month Year of access.

If the blog doesn't have a name, use the generic label Online Posting. If publisher or sponsor name is not available use n.p.

> Hampton, Frances. "16 ways to leave your lover." *My blog about love.* n.p. 13 Jan. 2009. Web. 12 Dec 2010. <http:/www.myblogaboutlove.com>.

APA (American Psychological Association)

APA style citation is widely used for social studies subjects. It was most recently updated in 2009, and this guide complies with that version.

In APA citation, works quoted or paraphrased in the text are followed by parenthetical citations comprised of the author name(s) and date (ex., Jones, 2009, p. 23). As in the MLA format, leave out whatever you put in the lead, such as the author name. Always include year with name, even in the lead. Example:

> According to Bonsal (1967), "Cubans welcomed actions aimed at reducing American influence" (266).

Page numbers are recommended but not required for paraphrased material, but are required for quoted material. Use footnotes only for describing the context of a citation or to acknowledge a copyright. However, overall, footnotes are discouraged. When citing the Internet, if the source is also available in print form, document it as though you had consulted the print version.

To list the works you used, start a new page, and center the word "References" at the top. Put the items in alphabetical order, ignoring "A," "An," and "The" at the beginning. Double space all entries and use hanging indent for each. Do not spell out first names; instead, use initials. Note that for periodicals, article title words are not put into caps except for the first word and proper names.

Sample APA Reference Entries

Books

Author, A. A. (Year of publication). *Title of work: Subtitle*. Location: Publisher.

Friedman, T. L. (2008). *Hot, flat and crowded: Why we need a green revolution—and how it can renew America*. New York, NY: Farrar, Straus and Giroux.

Article in Book

Author, A. A., & Author, B. B. (Year of publication). Title of chapter. In A. Editor & B. Editor (Eds.), *Title of book* (pp. pages of article). Location: Publisher.

Note: include "pp." before the numbers: (pp. 1–21) for articles in books and newspapers, but not for periodicals.

Wurdemann, J. G. F. (2004). A Physician's notes on Cuba. In A. Chomsky, B. Carr, and P. M. Smorkaloff (Eds.), *The Cuba reader: History, culture, politics* (pp. 39–43). Durham, NC: Duke University Press.

Journal Article

Author, A. A., Author, B. B., & Author, C. C. (Year). Title of article. *Title of Periodical*, volume number(issue number), pages.

Victor, D.G. and Yueh, L.(2010). The new energy order: managing insecurities in the twenty-first century. *Foreign Affairs*, 89(1), 61–73.

Magazine Article

Singing a different tune. (2009, Nov 12) *The Economist,* 73–74.

Online Source

Author, A. A., & Author, B. B. (Date of publication). Title of article. *Title of Online Periodical,* volume number (issue number if available). Retrieved from http://www.urladdress.com

APA uses a DOI (digital object identifier), when available, in place of the URL.

Garber, K. (2009, March 20). The green energy economy: What it will take to get there. *U.S. News & World Report*, 146 (3), 12. Retrieved from http://politics.usnews.com

Web Page

Author, A. A., & Author, B. B. (Date of publication). *Title of site.* Retrieved from http://Web address or DOI

Narey, W. (2006, Aug 2). Elizabethan worldview. *Luminarium.* Retrieved from http://www.luminarium.org

Image

Artist last name, artist first name. (artist's role– i.e. Artist, Architect). (Date of work). *Title* [object type]. Repository, City. Retrieved from http://url

Diebenkorn, Richard (Artist). (1955). *Berkeley No. 52* [painting], National Gallery of Art, Washington, DC. Retrieved from www.nga.gov.

Blog

Lastname, FirstInitial. (year, month day). Title of individual blog entry [Web log message]. Retrieved from http://www.blog.com

Hampton, F. (2009, January 13). 16 ways to leave your lover [Web log message]. Retrieved from http://www.myblogaboutlove.com

CMS (Chicago Manual of Style)

The Chicago Manual of Style uses two different formats, one that most humanities papers use, which is a fully cited footnote and a bibliography that essentially repeats that information, and another, preferred by science and social sciences, which is similar to the APA style with the exception that the "p." is left out of the page number (Jones 2009, 42). The examples here are the humanities, or footnote type. The reference to the source would be followed by a superscript number matching the footnote at the bottom of the page. Below are the formats for the footnote and the accompanying bibliography entry. For electronically published books, add the edition at the end of the citation (Kindle edition or PDF e-book, for example). Note that unlike MLA or APA entries, CMS entries are not indented.

Book

Footnote:

1. Firstname Lastname, *Title of book* (Place of publication: Publisher, year published), page number.

Bibliography:

Lastname, Firstname. *Title of book*. Place of publication: Publisher, year published.

Footnote:

1. Thomas L. Friedman, *Hot, Flat and Crowded: Why We Need a Green Revolution—and How It Can Renew America* (New York, NY: Farrar, Straus and Giroux, 2008), 43.

Bibliography:

Friedman, Thomas L. *Hot, Flat and Crowded: Why We Need a Green Revolution—and How It Can Renew America*. New York, NY: Farrar, Straus and Giroux, 2008.

Article in Book

Footnote:

1. John G. F. Wurdemann, "A Physician's Notes on Cuba," in *The Cuba Reader: History, Culture, Politics,* ed. Aviva Chomsky, Barry Carr,

and Pamela Maria Smorkaloff (Durham, NC: Duke University Press, 2004), 40.

Bibliography:

Wurdemann, John G. F. "A Physician's Notes on Cuba." In *The Cuba Reader: History, Culture, Politics,* edited by Aviva Chomsky, Barry Carr, Pamela Maria Smorkaloff, 39–43. Durham, NC: Duke University Press, 2004.

Magazine Article

Footnote:

1. "Singing a Different Tune," *The Economist* November.14–20, 2009, 73.

Bibliography:

"Singing a Different Tune." *The Economist,* November 14–20, 2009.

Journal Article

Footnote:

1. David G. Victor and Linda Yueh, "The New Energy Order: Managing Insecurities in the Twenty-first Century," *Foreign Affairs* 89, no.1 (2010): 65.

Bibliography:

Victor, David G. and Linda Yueh. "The New Energy Order: Managing Insecurities in the Twenty-first Century." *Foreign Affairs* 89, no.1 (2010): 61–73.

Web Source

Footnote:

1. Firstname lastname, "Title of web page," *Publishing organization or name of web site*, Publication date if available, URL, date accessed.

Bibliography:

Lastname, Firstname. "Title of web page." *Publishing organization or name of web site*. Publication date if available. URL.

Footnote:

1. Wayne Narey, "Elizabethan Worldview," *Luminarium*, 2 Aug 2006, http://www.luminarium.com (2 Feb 2010).

Bibliography:

Narey, Wayne. "Elizabethan Worldview." *Luminarium*. 2 Aug 2006. http://www.luminarium.com.

Image

Footnote:

Artist first name, artist last name, *Title of Work*, year of work.

Bibliography:

Artist's name, *Title of Work*, Date. Medium, Dimensions. Housing institution or collection.

Footnote:

1. Richard Diebenkorn, *Berkeley No. 52*, 1955.

Bibliography:

Diebenkorn, Richard. *Berkeley No. 52*. 1955. Oil on canvas, 148.9 × 136.8 cm. National Gallery of Art, Washington, DC. nga.gov. Web. 2 Feb. 2010.

Blog

Footnote:

Author first name, Artist last name. Title of work. Year.

Bibliography:

Author last name, Author first name. "Title." *Title of site*. Personal blog. URL (acessed mon day, year).

Footnote:

1. Frances Hampton. 16 ways to leave your lover. 2009.

Bibliography:

Hampton, Frances. "16 ways to leave your lover." *myblogabloutlove*. personal blog. http://www.myblogaboutlove.com (accessed Dec. 12, 2010).

CSE (Council of Science Editors)

The CSE or Council of Science Editors citation system can be somewhat frustrating to use, as it allows many different citation formats, and different science journals have their own idiosyncrasies of CSE formatting. There are three official versions: the name-year (N-Y), method, the citation-sequence (C-S) method, and the citation-name (C-N) method. In the name-year (N-Y) method, the in-text citation is given in parentheses at the end of the sentence; references appear in alphabetical order. In the citation-sequence (C-S) method, each time the reference is cited in the text, a superscript [1] appears. The first reference used is assigned a superscript of [1] and citations are numbers as they are used. When citing more than one source, include each superscript [1 2 3]. The sources are then listed in order of first use in the reference list. In the citation-name (C-N) method, superscripts are also used, but they refer to the numbers assigned to the sources listed in the references, which are in alphabetical order. The name-year reference (N-Y) is a parenthetical citation (name, date) with an alphabetical reference section. The formatting of the sources in reference list is otherwise the same for all three methods.

The examples below use the name-year (N-Y) method. In-text references appear in parentheses without commas (Friedman 2010). When necessary, add the month of publication to distinguish multiple works by the same author in the same year. CSE does not indent entries on the reference list.

Books

Author, AA. Year of publication. Title of work: Capitalize letter of first word only. Location: Publisher. # of pgs p.

Friedman, TL. 2009. Hot, flat and crowded 2.0: why we need a green revolution—and how it can renew America. New York, NY: Farrar, Straus and Giroux. 528 p.

Article/Chapter in Book

Author, AA. Author, BB. Year of publication. Title of chapter/article. In: Editor name A, Editor B, editors. Title of book. Nth ed. Location: Publisher. P. page range.

Wurdemann, JGF. 2004. A physician's notes on Cuba. In: Chomsky A, Carr B, Smorkaloff PM, editors. The Cuba reader: history, culture, politics. Durham, NC: Duke University Press. p. 39–43.

Journal Article

Author AA, Author BB, Author CC. Year. Title of article. Title of periodical, volume number(issue number): pages.

Use abbreviations where possible for journal names.

Victor DG, Yueh L. 2010. The new energy order: managing insecurities in the twenty-first century. For Affairs. 89(1): 61–73.

Magazine Article

Singing a different tune. 2009 Nov 12. The Economist. 73–74.

Online Source

Author, AA, Author BB. Date of publication. Title of article. Title of Online Periodical [Internet]. [cited year mon day]; volume number (issue number if available):pages. Available from: http://www.urladdress. com doi

Include a DOI (digital object identifier), when available.

Garber K. 2009 Mar 20. The green energy economy: what it will take to get there. U.S. News & World Rpt [Internet]. [cited 2010 Dec 12]; 146 (3):12. Available from: http://politics.usnews.com

Web Page

Author, AA, Author BB. Update date. Title of document. [Internet]. Title of site: [cited year mon day]. Available from: http://www.urladdress. com DOI if available

Narey W. 2006 Aug 2. Elizabethan worldview. [Internet]. Luminarium. [cited 2010 Dec 12]. Available from: http://www.luminarium.org

Image

Artist AA. Date of work. Title. [object type]. Repository. Location. [cited year mon day]. Available from: http://www.urladdress.com

Diebenkorn, R. 1955. Berkeley No. 52. [Painting]. National Gallery of Art, Washington DC. [cited 2010 Dec 2]. Available from: www.nga.gov.

Blog

Author AA. Title of post. In: http://www.urladdress.com [web blog] year mon day; [cited year mon day]. #pgs p.

Hampton F.16 ways to leave your lover. In: http://www.myblogaboutlove. com [web blog]. 2009 Jan. 13; [cited 2010 Dec. 12]. 1 p.

8

DEVELOPING STYLE

8.1 Eloquence

I have to come into my strength; words obey my call. —*William Butler Yeats*

What Yeats celebrated, you too can celebrate: the feeling of having a wide range and scope of language at your command. Indeed, this is what teachers evaluate when they evaluate style. They look for signs of a confident person writing with courage and pleasure. In developing your style of writing, you want to keep your own distinctive voice but raise it to a higher level of elegance, intensifying it to a higher register. Your focus should not be on trying to impress but on trying to convey your ideas and yourself in the best light—as you would present yourself at a fancy dinner party. Beware of the temptation to employ lofty-sounding language, as this strategy can obscure your voice and your purpose. Be your best-dressed self, not your overdressed self.

It's easier to demonstrate stylish writing than it is to tell how to accomplish it. Consider this passage:

Indonesia had been entered into Guinness World Records for having the fastest rate of deforestation in the world. Indonesia is now losing tropical forests the size of Maryland" every year, and the carbon released by the cutting and clearing of all these trees—much of it done illegally—has made Indonesia the third-largest source of greenhouse gas emissions in the world, after the United States and China. Brazil is number four for the same reason. We tend to think of the climate issue as purely an energy problem—how do we reduce the number of gasoline cars we drive and the amount of coal we burn? But in Indonesia, climate is a forest problem. We think of the problem as being too many cars. They think of it as being too few trees. More than 70 percent of CO2 emissions from Indonesia come from the cutting and clearing of forests. According to Conservation International, a forest area the size of three hundred soccer fields is cut down in Indonesia every hour. (Thomas Friedman, *Hot, Flat, and Crowded: Why We Need a Green Revolution—and How It Can Renew America*)

In his books and articles, journalist Thomas Friedman condenses complex, knotty problems into bite-sized, memorable analogies. And somehow, this way of turning phrases makes problems seem solvable, a worthy goal for any writer. Friedman's diction is simple—mostly one and two-syllable words. Yet the paragraph achieves a lot of thinking work. For one thing, it translates abstract numbers into easily imagined visuals: losing "three hundred soccer fields" of forest per hour, and cutting down tropical forests the "size of Maryland" every year. These images create mental pictures that dry statistics cannot convey. Friedman also uses a simple grammatical structure—parallelism—-to recast the environmental issue from an "energy problem" to a "forest problem," and from a concern over "too many cars" to the more devastating concept of "too few trees," as he compares "we" to "them." Other sentences aid the reader by placing important information either first or last, and non-essential information between dashes, like a verbal aside. Friedman's clear, direct, straight-talking style is worthy of emulation.

The next piece has a more conspicuously stylistic approach:

I feel some hesitation to invite you to come with me into the body. It seems a reckless, defiant act. Yet there is more than dread reflected from these rosy coasts, these restless estuaries of pearl. And it is time to share it, the way the catbird shares the song which must be a joy to him and is a living truth to those who hear it. So shall I make of my fingers, words; of my scalpel, a sentence; of the body of my patient, a story.

One enters the body in surgery, as in love, as though one were an exile returning at last to his hearth, daring uncharted darkness in order to reach home. Turn sideways, if you will, and slip with me into the cleft I have made. Do not fear the yellow meadows of fat, the red that sweats and trickles where you step. Here, give me your hand. Lower between the beefy cliffs. Now rest a bit on the peritoneum. All at once, gleaming, the membrane parts...and you are *in*. (Richard Seltzer, "The Surgeon as Priest")

If you sense both reverence and sexual enticement in this gorgeous passage, you are spot on. Selzter, a writer-surgeon, delights in describing the hushed spiritual awe he feels as he cuts into the human body. From his surprising yet instantly captivating metaphors ("estuaries of pearl" is so lovely that one doesn't even care if any part of the body resembles it) to the formal, almost biblical register of the prose, Selzter takes the reader to another, most amazing world. He is a writer who revels in ornate style, perfect for the pitch of reverence he feels and hopes to inspire. It's an inspiring passage to read whenever you experience writer's block.

In both excerpts, you can see that the author has taken Emerson's idea of finding "three or four stubborn necessary words" that capture the heart of the topic. It is not just a matter of adopting a style but of using language to foreground the central concepts.

Here is a student example:

How can we guard against the manipulative influence of advertisements? The most basic way is to remember to put intelligence before impulse: to stop, take stock, and rationally examine the ads that draw our attention. If the claim seems impossible, it probably is. If the statistics sound extreme, you might want to raise your eyebrows. If the product is promoted by a pretty model wearing designer clothes, you might question its authenticity. Simple skepticism is all we have as a tool against corporations that seek to exploit our insecurities, but it's all we need. Their ads spook and scare and distort and lie, but we are not powerless. Influence happens in our own minds and we have the power to reject it.

This student writes with clarity and verve. Note the effectiveness of the assonance of "intelligence before impulse" and the list, "to stop, take stock, and rationally examine." The growing length of the phrases mirrors the slowing-down process being recommended. The way the sentences are balanced ("skepticism is all we have...but it's all we need") create a sense of clarity, purposefulness and completeness, suggesting: here is truth, so act on it.

The next passage comes from a student's definition essay:

> "African" is a term that allows people to compress a complex group of people into a nice, bite-sized identity. Such a word cannot adequately define a person, yet it presumes to do so. I was born and raised for some time in Ethiopia, yet I hardly know all the rich and varied traditions, culture, and history of my heritage. And if the richness of heritage from one country is overwhelming, how much moreso is that of the totality of the fifty-three diverse, unique other countries that comprise the vast continent of Africa? The wealth of culture, tradition, language, and history in the aggregate experience of these fifty-three countries cannot be encapsulated in the restrictively vague term, "African." Worse, this word's insufficiency reduces the complexity of a person to a muddled amalgamation of misconceptions, rather than empowering him to embrace his ethnicity. Calling someone "African" not only oversimplifies a complex culture, it strips away the history of a person and undermines his very selfhood. Therefore, the term "African" should be thrown into the dustbin of history, along with other such misleading terms as "Nubian" and "Oriental."

This piece uses a number of stylistic techniques to convey the seriousness of the topic with an appropriate formality and directness, matching the register of the language to the importance of the content. Notice the repetition of three key words—traditions, culture, and history—that lie at the heart of this writer's concern about identity and labeling. The repetition of the number of African countries drives home her point that there are too many heritages in Africa to dismiss them with the single word "African." The alliteration and assonance of the last few sentences (the m's, the e's, the c's, the s's) carries the formality to a higher pitch, fitting for a final ringing truth.

A number of these writers made effective use of parallel structure, in which coordinated ideas have coordinated sentence format, like this:

> With this faith, we will be able to hew out of the **mountain of despair** a **stone of hope**. (Martin Luther King)

The elegance and majesty of King's sentence derives from the grammatical parallel between "mountain of despair" and "stone of hope." Here is another elegant use of parallelism, this time from former U.S. President, Bill Clinton:

> People the world over have always been more impressed by the **power of our example** than by the **example of our power**.

Notice the simplicity of the language. These are not big, impressive-sounding words, yet the sentence rings with dignity. The reversal of "power of example" to "example of power" is the centerpiece idea, and it is this reversal that lends the sentence its formality and grandeur. The format comes to us from ancient Greece, and even has a fancy Greek name—it's called an antimetabole. Here are two student examples of antimetabole, modeled on Clinton's example:

> The Supreme Court must create **justice without politics** or it will reap **politics without justice**.

> So far, we have had several major **failures of intelligence**; now we must gain **intelligence from our failures**.

Lovely, aren't they? And they impresses without signs of strain or effort. There are many other structured sentence patterns that have come down to us from ancient Greek times that allow a writer to present ideas with clarity and grace. You cannot go far wrong in modeling your sentences on classical Greek forms. There are plenty of examples available, in books and web pages of rhetorical figures of speech, and in famous speeches.

Style is the culmination of such choices in diction, tone, pacing, sentence structure, and organization. Since there exists no magic formula for improving style, start by paying attention to your choices and deliberately experimenting with new ones. While reading, notice the style choices other writers have made—those that work and those that do not. Implement one or two interesting turns of phrase or new vocabulary every time you write. You will soon see a big difference in the power of your writing.

Savvy writers also change their tone and level of formality to fit the occasion. This is because your style of writing conveys not only your ideas but also establishes your ethos, what the reader perceives as the character or persona of the narrator. In writing as in speaking, this means formal (but not flowery) language for formal occasions, bold (but not crude) language for persuasive essays, thoughtful (but not meandering) language for reflective pieces, jaunty (but not careless) language for informal chats. In other words, it requires following Hamlet's advice to a group of stage actors, to "fit the action to the word and the word to the action."

Here is an example (speaking of Hamlet), of language that does not fit its subject:

> *Hamlet* is chock full of misogyny: hatred of women. All the women are wimps who cannot even speak for themselves, let alone act for themselves. The worst one is Gertrude. She was definitely out of bounds when she married her husband's brother with "most wicked speed," a form of incest (1.2.158). Hamlet yells that she is "a beast that wants discourse of reason" (1.2.152). This drives Hamlet insane, so that he insults Ophelia, whom he once loved, and tells her to "get thee to a nunnery" (1.3.1), which the audience would know is a whorehouse.

Okay, the example is a bit over-the-top, but you get the idea. Is the diction appropriate for an academic essay? Has the writer created a credible ethos? Does the writing demonstrate control over language? In the revised passage below, the same writer displays more formality and precision, establishing his credibility and creating a plausible argument.

> Misogyny is rampant throughout *Hamlet*. Women are portrayed as a frail, weak, and base. It is not insignificant that the central events of the play cascade from Gertrude's betrayal and immediate remarriage. For overstepping the boundaries established by a patriarchal society, Gertrude is compared unfavorably to "a beast that wants discourse of reason" (1.2.152). Hamlet shows no mistrust of or disdain for women before her "incestuous" marriage (1.2.159); in fact, he had professed his love to Ophelia on more than one occasion. All this changes with Gertrude's marriage which took place with "most wicked speed" (1.2.158). Hamlet's sudden rejection of Ophelia seems directed not at her, but at all women, as he insults her with invectives against women's frailty and their inability to remain faithful to their husbands.

In the revised version, the writer has improved his vocabulary (without sounding pretentious and without misusing words) and has clarified and legitimized his point that women are presented in an unfavorable in *Hamlet*. He has raised the register of his writing to match the occasion, a serious critique of the play, and has shown himself to be a serious, careful thinker.

Summing Up

Eloquence consists in identifying the core ideas at the heart of your topic, architecting phrases and sentences to express those concepts in a balanced and structured manner, and keeping most of the vocabulary simple and clear, yet precise. Consider forming your most important sentences in parallel grammatical phrases and clauses to "dress up" your message beautifully. And fit the language to the purpose, making the expression suitable for the topic.

To write eloquently:

- Use balanced and parallel phrasing
- Keep it simple
- Model sentences on classic structures
- Create a credible ethos
- Fit diction and tone to the occasion
- Use precise, not pretentious, vocabulary

8.2 Concision

If you have ever wondered why a teacher gets slightly irritable when asked "how many pages should this be?" then you need to read this deliberately brief section. Teachers know the question often masks a mistaken tendency to prioritize quantity over quality. When your teacher replies, "write just enough to prove your point," she is not being glib, she means: write a bold, concise essay and do not demonstrate your anxiety by padding it out with fluff. Your reader should not have to wade through a lot of filler to get to your point. To prove your point thoroughly yet efficiently, make sure every word in the essay has a reason to be there. However, when writing your first draft, go ahead and get your thoughts onto paper without worrying too much about the wording. You don't want to slow down the flow of ideas to get the perfect wording on the first draft. But make sure to leave plenty of time to revise and improve the draft.

Here is a fairly typical first draft of a paragraph from an essay on Gerard Manley Hopkins' poem, "God's Grandeur":

> The second stanza makes a very deliberate shift from the completely oppressive gloom of the first, clearly introducing the birth of hope. The author gives examples of mankind's lost state. He knows that mankind has the potential to find its way back to the golden path from which it has erroneously strayed. He wants to offer hope that mankind can move forward in life, as though the bright morning that appears at the edge of "the brown brink eastward…" magnificently represents mankind's ultimate opportunity to break free of the horrible despair of the first stanza. Hope and promise of renewed faith and spiritual belief for all of mankind will come with the "spring" of the bright morning, "the brown brink eastward." Men will know that greatness awaits them. This great leap of faith will be protected by a holy loving father, God, as represented by the "Holy Ghost" who "over the bent world broods…" The poet has gone from a state of depression and gloom to one where he is full of hope and expressing signs of joy.

This paragraph contains plenty of quoted evidence and is on the right track, but the ideas lack clarity. Some of the writing detracts from the main point: that the poem shifts from a state of gloom to one of hope. The topic sentence should state this outright, and the rest should be streamlined to support it. Too much cutting, however, would remove the heart of the paragraph:

> The second stanza shifts from gloom to hope. Morning, "the brown brink eastward…" symbolizes mankind's new faith. Mankind can "spring" forth to spiritual renewal, overwatched by the "Holy Ghost" himself, bringing joy to the world.

Making a text concise and accurate is an art in itself. You can start by eliminating extra words and phrases, so that you get the piece down to its core ideas. So, let's first cross out redundant statements and extraneous modifiers:

> The second stanza ~~makes a very deliberate~~ shift from the ~~completely oppressive~~ gloom of the first, ~~clearly~~ introducing ~~the birth of~~ hope. ~~The author gives examples of mankind's lost state. He knows that mankind has the potential to find its way back to the golden path from which it has erroneously strayed.~~ He wants to offer hope ~~that mankind can move forward in life~~, as though the bright morning that appears at the edge of "the brown brink eastward…" ~~magnificently~~ represents mankind's ~~ultimate~~ opportunity to break free of the ~~horrible~~ despair of the first stanza. Hope and promise of renewed faith and spiritual belief for all of mankind will come with the "spring" of the bright morning, "the brown brink eastward." ~~Men will know that greatness awaits them.~~ This great leap of faith will be protected by a holy loving father, God, as represented by the "Holy Ghost" who "over the bent world broods…" The poet has gone ~~from a state of depression and~~ gloom to ~~one where he is full of hope and expressing signs of~~ joy.

Now it's easier to see the main ideas and to tune up the topic sentence. Once that is done, the evidence should support it, and in this case, it does. Now the writer can simply combine what is left into a more compact and still meaningful version:

> The second stanza makes a clear shift from the gloom of the first, introducing the birth of hope, a path back to faith. Morning appears at the edge of "the brown brink eastward…" symbolizing mankind's opportunity to break free of the worldly monotony of to "have trod, have trod, have trod" in "trade," such that they have lost their spirituality as well as their spirit. But now, declares Hopkins, mankind can "spring" forth to spiritual renewal. And this leap of faith will be protected by a loving "Holy Ghost" who "over the bent world broods…" The realization that the Holy Ghost cares about the state of man fills the poet, and reader, with joy.

This paragraph is about half as long, but is twice as effective as the first draft. The language now conveys the writer's confident interpretation of a difficult yet rewarding poem.

Consider now a different kind of conciseness problem: taking too long to get to the point:

> The socio-economic status of Cuba was not bad enough to ignite a people's revolution alone. However, the social factors in Cuba were not perfect, and certain social patterns arose under Batista that exacerbated the level of unrest to the socio-economic scene in Cuba. One of the social patterns that exposed Cuba to some level of social unrest was the intermittent migration of farmers and rural workers to urban areas and cities during the ebbs and flows of the sugar harvest cycle.

In this case, the sentences don't do enough work: they simply list some of the problems in Cuba before Castro's revolution. The writer needs to rethink what he is trying to say. Once he synthesizes the ideas, he discovers that he first needs to make a concession, then state his premise. The whole paragraph can actually be stated in one concise sentence:

> Although socio-economic conditions in Cuba before the revolution were difficult for farmers and workers due to the ebbs and flows of the sugar harvest cycle, the situation was not bad enough on its own to ignite a revolution.

Many young writers throw in extra adjectives and adverbs in an attempt to dress up their prose. But this can be like sewing a bunch of different fancy collars and pockets onto a shirt. Your sentences will be more elegant with a simpler style of dress. Strong writers also learn to strip away their most precious words—the ones that sparkle so much that they succeed only in communicating pretentiousness—to achieve clarity. But the most important means of achieving clarity is to have thought through the ideas and to have decided what points to make and in what order, before starting to write.

Summing Up

Concision means getting to the point quickly, stating the main point clearly and early, and stripping away unnecessary words and phrases to leave just those needed to develop an idea. So plan ahead, but when writing your draft, silence your inner editor to allow your thoughts to flow, allowing adequate time afterwards to trim and revise it for clarity and concision.

To achieve concision:

- Brainstorm to identify key concepts
- Compress ideas to essentials
- Get to the point quickly
- Remove redundant and flowery language
- Keep it simple and bold
- Plan ahead and allow time for editing

8.3 Clarity

Writing instructors sometimes send mixed messages about clarity, encouraging brevity on one hand and thoroughness and precision on the other. These two goals seem contradictory, but in the best writing, both are accomplished. Yes, you want to trim out extraneous words and repeated ideas, and yes, you need to develop ideas fully and use precise language to make your meaning clear. Like the sculptor, you must trim away the excess material in order to reveal the beautiful and intricately designed work inside. Your goal is not to impress, but to communicate effectively. This section focuses on what you can do to strike a successful balance between brevity and clarity, so that your ideas shine forth. You can express complex ideas clearly if you order your sentences logically.

The first thing to think about, before committing yourself to sentences that turn to concrete and are hard to revise, is your **main idea,** the "who, what, where, and when," and the **point**, which tells "why." There is no substitute for knowing what you are talking about before you say it.

In the following passage, each sentence makes sense, but the main idea and the point are not at all clear:

> Signs of dissatisfaction in the sugar industry workers were visible. Castro saw this so his message was received by the Cuban people.

The growth of Cuban ownership of some businesses in the world of sugar was another issue. Another issue was the imperialism, which was from the United States. Castro wanted the U.S. out and he wanted to nationalize the sugar industry and the Cubans agreed.

This writer has a grasp of some of the problems in Cuba, but seems unsure about why she is talking about them. After some free-writing and thinking to identify her main point (that conditions in Cuba were ripe for Castro's appeal to nationalize the sugar industry), she restructured her paragraph. Here's her improved version:

Conditions were ripe in Cuba for nationalization. This is because on one hand, the people didn't realize there was economic growth and increased Cuban ownership of businesses, although on the other hand they realize that the sugar industry workers were dissatisfied. So Castro convinced them to nationalize the sugar industry.

The version above improves clarity by providing a topic sentence and framing the other information as contributing causes. However, the language is passive, not indicating who is the **actor**, the person or entity doing something. She has a choice of actors, here, between Castro and the Cuban people. Her main point is that Castro capitalized on the confusion over the economy and social conditions to nationalize the sugar industry. She decides to cast the problem in terms of the people and make them the actor. In the following version, this point is clearer, because the writer puts the actor into the subject of the first sentence:

The Cubans were drawn to Castro's solution to nationalize the sugar industry and to free themselves of U.S. imperialist involvement because they saw visible and disturbing unrest in the sugar industry workers and at the same time the slow but steady growth of the Cuban economy—especially the growth of Cuban-owned businesses—was invisible to them.

Notice that the reasons appear in a "because" clause, with an aside that mentions one less crucial reason, so that the main idea can stand alone in the grammatical spotlight. This arrangement clarifies that the **actor**

is the Cuban people. Notice the difference in actors between these two
sentences:

> The general sent the brigade up the mountain to take out the
> enemy's advanced guard.

> The brigade took out the enemy's advanced guard.

The choice of subjects here would depend on the topic of the essay,
whether it is about the general or about the brigade. Remember that the
subject does not have to appear in the first few words. An introductory
modifier can provide additional context without detracting from the
reader's understanding of the point:

> Having completed their training, the brigade carried out the
> general's command to take out the enemy's advanced guard.

Or:

> Despite the mud and snow, the brigade carried out the general's
> command to take out the enemy's advanced guard.

Clarity is achieved when your sentences clearly indicate the actor and
main action in the subject and verb. But that does not mean writing
a series of subject-verb-object sentences. The context, causes, reasons,
and conditions of the action should instead be structured in subordinate
clauses and phrases.

The following string of grammatically simple sentences actually obscures
the intended meaning:

> Socrates outlined a very specific arts education curriculum for
> the guardians and noted that to veer from the proscribed path
> would cause illness in either the soul or the body, or both.
> They must be taught exactly which luxuries are necessary and
> which are not. Guardians must be taught music and gymnastics,
> in this order, so that their souls do not become too soft or too
> hard (69).

The main idea is that the guardians need to learn which arts are crucial
and which are luxuries, but this idea gets lost in the wordy sentences

above. To clarify it, combine the sentences using subordinate clauses and phrases:

> Socrates insisted that the guardians be trained in the crucial arts of music and gymnastics, which would strengthen their souls, and be warned to avoid the other arts, for indulging those luxuries could cause illness of the soul or body (69).

At times you will want to tune your subject, using concrete, specific nouns: not "the general," but "General Patton"; not "a mountain," but "the Ardennes." Or, you may want to zoom in for a closer perspective, as in the difference between these two sentences:

> The drummer kept up a steady, driving beat.
> His drumsticks tattooed a driving rhythm.

In the second sentence, the action, not the drummer, deliberately gets center stage, creating a strong visual and aural image. Notice the verb choices as well. "Tattooed" evokes a vivid image that also displays the writer's ingenuity and joy in writing. It's the difference between saying "walk" when you mean "stagger" or "swagger." Of course, one does need to resist the temptation to jazz up a sentence in a confusion of disparate images and tones.

Summing Up

To write clearly, you first must decide what it is you want to say. That sounds easy, but too often writers work their way to their main idea instead of beginning with it. Once again, free-writing can help clarify your thoughts. Then, decide what order to present them in by asking yourself why you are including each point. Once you develop a plan, structure sentences to put the driver in the driver's seat, so to speak— with the actor as the subject. Some details deserve primary placement, some are side issues. Put them into sentences according to their status. A side issue can appear in an introductory phrase, or as a modifier of a more important idea. Think of which ideas you would throw overboard in a sinking ship, and put those into subordinate positions in the sentences, if not into the water.

To write with clarity:

- Before writing, identify the main points to be made

- Put main points into the topic sentences of each paragraph

- Order the ideas within the paragraph logically

- Structure sentences with the actor as the subject

- Use precise verbs

- Use transitional phrases to guide the reader

- Put contextual information into modifying phrases and clauses

- Combine sentences using subordinate clauses that indicate priority

- Decide when to zoom in or out

Attaining wisdom in any activity involves making some mistakes along the way. Writing is no different. Style is so personal, elusive, and multifaceted that all writers can expect to make some missteps along the way to fluency and control. The most talented artists, athletes, and musicians will agree that part of the process of learning advanced skills includes flashes of brilliance alongside moments of clumsiness, of leaping forward, only to lose sight of the goal. And no one, no matter how accomplished, can magically tell you how to develop your style, though they can guide and sympathize. In the end, your style, your writing voice, will come from within you, as you experiment, discover, and build confidence.

9

AN OVERVIEW OF THE WRITING PROCESS

Here is a rough diagram of how a typical essay might be constructed. The lines represent logical connections that should be made (topic sentences connect to the thesis statement, and so on):

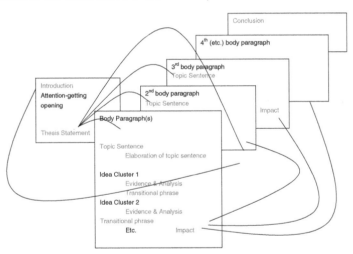

Here is a summary of the typical steps in writing an essay. Of course, "your mileage may vary," in that you may skip, combine, or add steps, depending on the type of essay you are writing. For more information about each step, see the chapter indicated.

1. Reading and Researching

    1.1 Annotating Texts: If your essay will discuss a text or texts, highlight things that are unusual, puzzling, or important, such as key concepts, and write a quick summary of events in the margin. Define, as best you can, difficult word or phrases. Also record your reaction in shorthand form.

1.2 Taking Notes: If you are using sources for information, take great care in distinguishing quoted material from your own words. Put quotation marks around all words taken directly from the source. Write the author and page number (and date or title for multiple works by one writer) after each passage. Put a full citation at the top of each page of notes from a given source. Alternatively, you might start a new page for each subtopic, being mindful to include a citation for different each piece of evidence. Start the works cited page immediately and keep it updated. Keep your working thesis literally in front of you as you read.

2. Generating Ideas

Go beyond the obvious to develop a thesis worth writing about. To find a compelling thesis, think deeply about the material. Consider what is not stated, what underlying assumptions exist, as well as implications and consequences. Think about what can be learned by considering the contributions of the speaker, the text, the audience, and the context.

Where sources disagree, which position seems most convincing? What other factors might be involved?

What main ideas and themes of the class are raised?

Consider what the writing prompt, if present, has asked. Determine whether you are to analyze, compare, define, or illustrate a topic. Write at least two difference possible thesis statements and then see which one will be more interesting to support with your findings.

3. Preparing to Write

3.1 Free-Writing: One of the best way to discover your own insights is to think by writing. Start anywhere, brainstorming ideas, and arguing with yourself. Allow enough time to delve into the topic in depth. When you feel like stopping, keep writing, as you often have a breakthrough in thinking just when you feel you have exhausted all of your ideas.

3.2 Organizing to Write: Often the best approach is a "details up" method where you sort and re-sort your ideas until a thesis and outline begin to come into focus. Some prefer to start with a thesis, but this method risks oversimplifying the topic.

The details-up method works well for large amounts of data for which you do not immediately see a logical outline. To derive one, arrange and re-arrange your evidence. Start by listing or placing all of your notes and evidence in front of you. Assign codes for categories of information (see page 42). Arrange the categories into order and play with the sequencing. What categories need more information? Which can be combined or eliminated?

Create a scratch outline and try putting your evidence into the outline. You may discover that more research is necessary for some subtopics.

3.3 Deriving a Thesis: A thesis is a sentence that is arguable yet supportable by evidence. It circumscribes the scope of the essay and provides the reader with a clear idea of where the essay will go. A too-broad thesis cannot be fully proven in the space of the essay. A too-narrow one might be obvious or unimportant. Usually the thesis answers a How or Why question.

4. Structuring the Essay

The format of the essay depends on the discipline for which it is written, as well as the content. Consider how you want to present your ideas. Is this a pro-con assessment? Are you describing causes and consequences, or are you narrating an event of describing or defining something? Will you need extensive corroborating evidence, or are you being asked to offer your own ideas? See Chapter 4.1 for a detailed list of possible essay structures. Remember that essays often combine two or more structural elements: a pro-con argument can be supported by cause-effect reasoning, narrative, description, or by classifying items, etc.

4.2 Introductions: Avoid sweeping, panoramic introductions (Since the dawn of time...) and instead capture the reader's attention with a provocative lead that directs attention to a legitimate idea or concern. Provide just enough background information to set up the thesis statement and to indicate the purpose of the essay.

The introduction should be general, but not too broad; specific, but not too narrow.

4.3 Body Paragraphs: Remember that the purpose of writing an essay for a class is to demonstrate how well you think about the topic. Structure the body paragraphs to support your thesis with compelling evidence and arguments. Each topic sentence, which is like a mini-thesis that governs the body paragraph, should link to and partially explain the thesis. Move smoothly from one idea to the next, incorporating quoted evidence into your own sentences. Develop ideas fully, but not in tedious detail. Use transitional words and phrases to guide the reader through the material. End the paragraph with an impact statement that leads to the idea to be developed in the next paragraph.

Body Paragraph(s)
Topic Sentence
Elaboration of topic sentence
Idea Cluster 1
Evidence & Analysis
Transitional phrase
Idea Cluster 2
Evidence & Analysis
Transitional phrase
Etc.
Impact

4.4 Conclusions: Avoid the temptation simply to repeat the thesis in the conclusion. This can bore the reader, who has just read your thesis in the introduction. Instead, send the reader off with a powerful message, eloquently expressed. Tie the thesis to larger implications about life, society, or human nature. Express a call to action, suggesting that the reader feel a sense of responsibility for taking action. Or return to a detail in the introduction, or to a key concept, which you now develop with greater understanding. In any event, end with a bold flourish, to delight your reader.

AFTERWORD

Writing is not a chemical formula with a perfect answer made up of nouns and verbs. Rather it is a process, a dance, a painting meant to capture a fleeting idea or an extraordinary moment and to share it with a reader. It is not a science, but an art that requires the artist to be willing to take risks. Write often. Create order to enhance understanding. Discover your ideas through writing. Develop them through writing. Many authors will attest to the need to go through draft after draft to discover what they want to say. So the best way for you to acquire new skills in organizing, developing, and expressing your ideas is to allow yourself to take writing risks, experimenting with language and structure. You will find that you will progress faster the more you allow yourself the freedom to explore and play with writing. Compare the early writing of any famous author with his later work, and you will see how much improvement comes with time and attention. No doubt, these writers had moments of frustration, but they persevered, as I hope you will, to unlock the joy of writing.

Recommended Reading

Harvey, Gordon. *Writing with Sources: A Guide for Students.* Indianapolis, IN: Hackett Publishing, Inc., 2008.

Harvey, Michael. *The Nuts and Bolts of College Writing.* Indianapolis, IN: Hackett Publishing, Inc., 2003.

McIrney, D. Q. *Being Logical: A Guide to Good Thinking.* New York, NY: Random House, 2005.

Quinn, Arthur and Barney R. Quinn. *Figures of Speech: 60 Ways to Turn a Phrase*. New York, NY: Routledge, 1995.

Williams, Joseph M. *Style: The Basics of Clarity and Grace, 3rd edition*. Boston, MA: Longman, 2008.

APPENDIX: SAMPLE ESSAYS

MLA Footnote Citation

The poem being analyzed in the essay
that follows is included for ease of
understanding the essay. It would not
necessarily be included in the actual
essay.

Yet Do I Marvel

I doubt not God is good, well-meaning, kind
And did He stoop to quibble could tell why
The little buried mole continues blind,
Why flesh that mirrors Him must some day die,
Make plain the reason tortured Tantalus
Is baited by the fickle fruit, declare
If merely brute caprice dooms Sisyphus
To struggle up a never-ending stair.
Inscrutable His ways are, and immune
To catechism by a mind too strewn
With petty cares to slightly understand
What awful brain compels His awful hand.
Yet do I marvel at this curious thing:
To make a poet black, and bid him sing!

Countée Cullen, 1925

Student Name
Course and Instructor Name
Date

Do Not Marvel

Few critics have been willing to see Countée Cullen's "Yet Do I Marvel" as anything beyond a defeated lament over the mixed blessing of being

> Poet name, name of poem appear in first line.

a talented artist in a racist society. The consensus is that the sonnet *blames* God for making him black and a poet. Rachel Blau Duplessis, in particular, claims that Cullen's poem "compound[s] the strength of black poetic authority by seeing it as an impossible test of authorship authorized by God himself."[1] However, Duplessis and others have misunderstood the poem. Although

> Writer makes a concession (Although racial identity...) and presents the thesis in the last two sentences of the introduction.

> Footnote for MLA citation.

racial identity and its struggles are faintly embedded in the last two lines, Cullen focuses more on rejecting the *stereotypes* associated with blackness, and perhaps even more generally encourages his readers to break free from the steel walls formed by *any* society's constructed norm. The theme of resistance to and appropriation of established norms is most apparent in the way that Cullen revises the genre of the Shakespearean sonnet, enriching it with sprung rhythms and unconventional rhyme schemes.

On the surface, the quatrains, couplets, and arcane language of the poem follow the format of the Shakespearean sonnet. However, Cullen does not allow himself to be bound by the traditional form, choosing instead to begin with two quatrains (as opposed to three) and end with three couplets (in place of a final one). He understands the rules but shows unfailing courage and abiding resolve in breaking them. In an era when black poets were not generally accepted, this makes a powerful statement about his personality: he will not "cease to sing" because of his race.

---

1 DuPlessis, Rachel Blau. *Genders, Races, and Religious Cultures in Modern American Poetry, 1908–1934.* Cambridge University Press, 2001. p. 115.

Cullen's audacity becomes more apparent when examining his rhyme scheme, where he demonstrates that he is not at all struggling with

> Topic sentence announces content of the paragraph.

an impossible task, as Duplessis so emphatically put it. His joy in embracing the marvel of his artistic gift can be seen in his playful use of sprung rhythm. The number of syllables and the stresses placed on them vary considerably; no two lines contain the expected rhymed pairings. Whereas each line in the Shakespearean sonnet is in end-stopped, iambic pentameter, Cullen's rhyme scheme bounces with enjambed lines and a jazz-like, unconventional rhythm. Thus we can take Cullen at his word when he

> Refer to author by last name or first and last name, never first name only.

says, "I doubt not God is good, well-meaning, kind." Rather than expressing sarcasm or irony, Cullen *does* in fact hold respect for God; he simply struggles to understand God's inscrutable ways. It is also interesting to note how Cullen ties his relationship with the deity to his overall message. The trend of negative terms such as "inscrutable, immune, petty, awful" transforms to joy in the final line where he proclaims that God "make[s] a poet black and bids him sing." If God can break from his own tradition, Cullen says, and we are made to mirror Him (line 4), then it is our *duty* to also follow this example.

> The last sentence in the paragraph explains the larger impact of the ideas.

Finally, the rhyme scheme breaks the sonnet mold as well. Just as we are beginning to get accustomed to Cullen's abab/cdcd scheme in lines 1 through 8, he abruptly switches to rhyming couplets: immune/strewn and understand/hand. The abab/cdcd/eeffgg scheme gives "Yet Do I Marvel" a unique variation on the traditional sonnet rhyme scheme. Again Cullen seems to lull the reader with an expected pattern in the beginning, only to purposely and abruptly shift it, demonstrating his poetic power.

Countee Cullen's "Yet Do I Marvel" primarily deals with the iron grip placed on minorities and those who are "different." *Yet* he revels, or "marvels" in being different, a black poet who has the courage to ignore the norm and sing. He persuades his audience to do the same.

> Conclusion expands thesis by applying it to the audience.

Comparison of Two Paintings

Student Name
Course and Instructor Name
Date

The Renewing Spirit of Renaissance Art

Madonna and Child
André Berlinghiero, c. 1230
Tempera on wood, gold ground,
80.3 × 53.7
Metropolitan Museum of Art,
New York

An Old Man and His Grandson
Domenico Ghirlandaio c. 1490
Tempera on wood, 62 × 46 cm
Louvre, Paris

http://en.wikipedia.org/wiki/File:Italo–Byzantinischer_Maler_des_13._Jahrhunderts_001.jpg

During the period of cultural blossoming in Europe known as the Renaissance, an undeniably distinct thought process was afoot in Italy. Craftsmen developed into artisans,

> The writer provides just enough historical background in the introduction.

altering traditional subjects and the style of expression to match the societal interest in studies that later became known as the "Humanities." Writers and artists alike turned away from the traditional subject of the church to focus on the individual, usually a wealthy one; they also incorporated elements of classical art, having rediscovered its beauty. One such artist, Domenico Ghirlandaio (1449–1494), a Florentine, painted a portrait of his own patron, an elderly individual, and entitled his work *An Old Man and His Grandson* (c.1480). Through

> Artwork titles are expressed in *italics*, not quotation marks.

this exemplary work of Renaissance art, he represents his patron in a loving pose with his grandson, something entirely secular and unlike the overwhelming majority of traditional religious paintings. His work is groundbreaking and yet also demonstrates significant connections with traditional religious works of art.

Tender portraits such as the one by Ghirlandaio simply do not exist among the paintings of the Middle Ages. A preponderance of Medieval paintings depict the Madonna, the Virgin Mary with her child, Jesus. In these images Mary holds an adult-looking Baby Jesus, the two awkwardly situated so as to avoid

> Comparison of traits.

any hint of intimacy. For example, see the Madonna and Child by André Berlinghiero, an Italian painter from Lucca (active by 1228; by 1236), pictured above. This painting displays Byzantine influences typical of the Medieval Madonna, with its standardized, angular faces, strong emotions, simple background, and rich but somber coloration. The baby Jesus's manlike appearance comes from the Medieval sense of honoring Jesus and thus refusing to display him as an innocent child. Mary stares away from her child as she supports him with one arm, maintaining a respectful distance from the holy child, and gestures towards him as the savior.

> Analysis is anchored in specific visual details.

Ghirlandaio's work deliberately recalls the Madonna portrait and portrays the influence of Byzantine coloration and simplicity, but in this case, the two related individuals have distinct personalities. They are seated in one eternal embrace. The child, in a very natural position for a grandson, sits comfortably and intimately in his grandfather's lap, his left hand reaching as far round his elder as possible. Their gaze reveals intimacy and a wealth of emotion.

Curiously the nose of the old man is deformed, most likely the result of disease, and there is a wart on his right temple. Both exemplify Ghirlandaio's Renaissance belief that people ought to be painted as realistically, and not as they once were or might wish to appear. Yet these human traits of the patron are not the first aspect to draw the viewer's eye. In fact one first notices the scarlet robe, then the tender face of the old man, the grandson's soft rosy-cheeked face, the landscape through the open window, and finally, once one really scrutinizes the painting, the man's deformities. These imperfections convey the defining human aspects of the individual.

> Analyzes where the eye is drawn.

Along with its turn toward the individual, the Renaissance constituted a revival of classical themes and artistic techniques. Ghirlandaio, too, demonstrates the influence of classical elements, but he refines them into something fresh and new. Classical art is dominated by geometric shapes, with the Golden Ratio apparent in many classical works; Ghirlandaio's geometric elements are more subtle: framed by the old man and his grandson, a rectangular window in turn, frames a soothing natural scene: a river winds from just behind the sill back beyond a tree and a hill to a rocky mountain. Had Ghirlandaio lived a hundred years earlier, during Medieval times, his painting would most certainly not have included a window let alone a surrounding countryside in his painting. Such an interest in classical ideals, including nature and orderly geometric figures, simply did not exist when Ghirlandaio's immediate artistic ancestors were painting, nor would they have ever achieved the physical depth present in *An Old Man and His Grandson*, from the child in the foreground to the distant mountain and beyond even to still further hills. In classical times, the geometric elements emphasized harmony and balance, but in Ghirlandaio's portrait, they offer a sense of time, suggesting the taking of one's place in the order of things.

> Contrasts the paintings' use of shapes.

Another innovation of the Renaissance compared to Medieval art lies in the use of color. From the intense red of the old man's robe to the hair and faces of the two individuals, varying hues create realistic human emotion, lovely folds in the cloth, and complex shadows cast by the setting sun through the window, all contributing depth and emotion. This use of striking contrasts in color and slight shading was certainly not demonstrated a couple of centuries earlier, as evidenced by all the flat, dark, non-secular paintings of that era.

Ghirlandaio unites his subjects through color, but more importantly, through emotion. He dressed his patron in a bright red robe, giving his young subject a skull cap of the same color. The color links them and draws the eye up toward the flesh of the elderly man. Then it follows his admiring gaze past his nose to the child's innocent eyes. Flowing from the youth's crown are delicate locks of blond hair, each strand of which the artist carefully curled. This idealization of the child was a new artistic theme of the Renaissance: the innocence and glory of the child. At the same time, the grandfather exhibits humanity, generosity, and the wisdom that comes with age. One sees his pride in and love for his grandson, as though simply holding him renews his own spirit.

From the repeated rectangles in the middle ground to the tenderness expressed between the two subjects, Domenico Ghirlandaio's *An Old Man and His Grandson* exhibits many of the hallmarks of the Renaissance. His respect for the beauty of nature, his command for the use of varied and contrasting color, and his attention to detail all contributing to a wonderfully intricate and yet elegant work of Italian Renaissance art. In all of these aspects, Ghirlandaio's painting echoes the Renaissance of the human spirit, a joy in life that it transmits to the viewer as well.

> Parallel structure (His respect... his command...his attention) adds formality and eloquence to the conclusion.

3   Science Research Essay

CSE Citation-Sequence Notation

Student Name
Course and Instructor Name
Date

Increased Complexity of Ammonite Sutures: Evidence of Evolution?

The ammonite, an extinct snail (cephalopod) is found in the fossil record beginning in the Devonian era, 416 to 359.2 million years ago, and ending in the Cretaceous–Paleogene (or K–Pg) extinction event 65 million years ago. Much like the Nautilus, the ammonite carries a spiral coiled shell and dwells within the body chamber, which is separated from the other chambers (phragmacones) by a thin membrane called the septal wall. It propels itself by pumping water through the chambers. A particularly interesting feature of the ammonites is the complex patterns of the sutures, the seam-like joint, along the septal margin, where the septum meets the shell wall. In many fossil ammonites, this margin area is visible as a suture line beneath the outermost shell layer.[1] Later species have suture lines that show greater complexity than earlier species,[1][2][3] which has triggered much debate about whether the complexity can be seen as an advancement, and thus a result of natural selection of superior traits, or a random evolution, and thus a passive event.[4]

Although complex sutures can be beneficial to the individual ammonite, greater complexity has no bearing on the overall evolutionary success of the class,[2] and therefore is not driven by natural selection but a passive

> Appropriate scientific terms are briefly defined.

> The superscript numbers refer to sources in the numbered reference list, which are listed in order of use. This is the "citation sequence" version of CMS notation.

trend resulting from increased diversity and variation over time. Furthermore, the benefits of complex suturing are not significant enough to give these members any evolutionary advantage over their simply sutured relatives; rather, each configuration has traits that would be beneficial or detrimental depending on the specific function or environment. The overall increase in suture complexity, then, is not a result of natural selection of superior traits but a simple expansion of species traits due to the success and abundance of the group as a whole. Ammonite suture development demonstrates that a progressive change in an attribute of a species, even when it benefits the species, is not necessarily the result of natural selection.

> Thesis appears at end of introduction.

While the functions of complex sutures have no bearing on the evolutionary success of the animal in the long term, these intricate septal margins can serve the creature well in life, namely, by providing greater area for muscle and body attachment, increased buoyancy control, and possibly greater resilience against hydrostatic pressure in deeper water levels, although this last point is highly disputed. The more complex the suturing, the larger the surface area, which means a large surface for muscle and body attachment despite the confined quarters of the body chamber. The greater the complexity of sutures, the stronger the anchor between body and shell, which is advantageous for both regular movement and capturing food (see figure below).[1 5] Complex suturing also provides increased buoyancy control due to the larger weight of the shell,[5] which gives the pelagic animal more control over its movements and an increased diving depth potential. The final, and perhaps most hotly debated, benefit of suture complexity is the supposed reinforcement of the shell by its internal saddles and lobes, which in turn greatly increases the amount of hydrostatic pressure the creature could endure.[3 5] However, a recent study suggests that suture complexity would result in extremely thin septal margins occurring at low angles, which would not "buttress" the shell, but in fact render it more vulnerable to hydrostatic pressure.[6] Further evidence shows that ammonites with simple sutures are therefore better suited to deep water living because their shells can withstand high hydrostatic pressures without risk of implosion.[4 6 7]

The benefits of complex sutures might have aided the animal in life, but would

> Clear topic sentence.

> The chart provides
> a helpful visual aid.

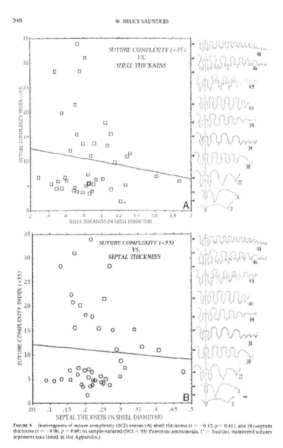

FIGURE 4. Scattergrams of suture complexity (SC2) versus (A) shell thickness ($r = -0.13$, $p = 0.41$) and (B) septum thickness ($r = -0.06$, $p = 0.68$) in simple-sutured (SC1 < 35) Paleozoic ammonoids. (* = Nautilus, numbered sutures represent taxa listed in the Appendix.)

not necessarily have led had an overall impact on species longevity. To accomplish species advancement, it would be necessary for the ammonite to continue to evolve based on the advancement of some trait such as suture complexity. However, in the case of ammonites, despite temporary benefits to the individual, there is no evidence suggesting that complex sutures are evolutionarily superior to the simple sutures with lower fractal dimensions.[2] Over time, those species of ammonoid with simple sutures show a much more constant success rate, and recent evidence suggests that a lower fractal dimension[A1] in the septal margin provides a greater capacity to endure high hydrostatic pressures. One of the main strengths of the simple sutured ammonites was their sheer capacity for survival—they lived through several mass extinction events that nearly obliterated all complex varieties, and throughout the ranges of various ammonite suture varieties, the simplest forms continue to exist.[4] Were complex sutures a factor in the success of ammonites, we can infer that simple forms would be eliminated by natural selection; however, this is not the case. Also, it is thought that perhaps the record of simpler forms would grow scarce as gradually they became obsolete, but this is not the case either—simple forms of ammonites with fractal dimensions approaching one are recurrent in the fossil record throughout the existence of the ammonites.[3] Overall, there does not seem to be any major difference in the evolutionary success rate between simple and complex suture forms.[2 3 8] In fact, a comparison chart of fractal dimension versus stratigraphic range shows the greatest concentrations of high taxonomic longevity are found between 1.2 and 1.3 in fractal dimension (See figure below) implying that neither extreme simplicity nor complexity would be advantageous, rather, those groups with moderate fractal dimensions are more likely to have generally greater longevity.

> Deductive reasoning: one claim leads logically to the next.

If complex sutures have no bearing on taxonomic longevity, then why the high proportion of complex forms? If not natural selection, then what causes the increase in and abundance of complex sutures while simpler forms coexist and continue? In part, the abundance of ammonites with fluted septal margins is simply a result

> Interesting but nonessential information is included in a footnote below.

[A1] The measure of fractal dimension, as employed by Boyajian and Lutz, serves as "a proxy for anatomical complexity," which is perhaps best described by the prolific scholar Stephen Jay Gould:

> Since a straight line has a fractal dimension of one, and a plane a fractal dimension of two, twisty lines must measure between one and two—that is, between a minimum of one for the straight line between two points, and the unattainable maximum of two for a line that twists and turns so much that it fills an entire plane between the two points at opposite edges. The higher the fractal dimension, the more "complex" the suture in our visceral and traditional sense that the squiggliest lines are the most elaborate.

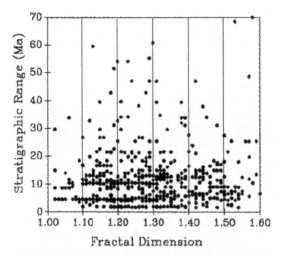

Figure 1: Taxonomical longevity versus suture complexity; shows no correlation between increased complexity and success, however, the general bell curve shape must be noted in addition to the high concentration of relatively long stratigraphic ranges for those ammonites whose fractal dimensions were between 1.20 and 1.30.

of the unidirectional growth potential. The least complex ammonites have a fractal dimension of almost one—a straight line. If this is the beginning point, the only potential for development would be a higher fractal dimension—the development of more complex septal margins. Increased complexity, then, is not a result of natural selection but of restricted growth potential. The only possible change is to become more complex, since fractal dimension cannot decrease past one. As Gould discusses, an increase in complexity gives no indicator of a driven trend or of natural selection—this movement towards the complex is simply a byproduct of initial "left wall orientation," so unidirectional growth is an inevitability, not an aim. This change is what Gould deems "an incidental effect of minimally simple beginnings at a left wall, followed by no bias whatever for increasing complexity in individual lineages thereafter."[3]

> In science essays, sources are usually not quoted.

According to the known evidence, the only explanation for the increased complexity of sutures remains with the "Left Wall of Minimal Complexity"[3] and the inevitable diversification of the species. Thus, the complexity of sutures is not, in fact, a desired trait of natural selection, but a random outcome stemming from natural differentiation, not evolution. In the search for evidence of evolution, the ammonite's suture patterns offer no conclusive evidence either for or against it.

References

1. Benton, M. J., Harper, D. A. T., Basic paleontology. Harlow, Essex, England: Longman; 1997. 360 p.

> CSE formatted reference list. Items are numbered in "citation sequence" format.

2. Boyajian, G. E., Lutz, T., Evolution of biological complexity and its relation to taxonimic longevity in the ammonoidea. Geology. 1992. 20: 983–986.

3. Gould, S. J., Full house : the spread of excellence from Plato to Darwin. New York: Three Rivers Press; 1997. 244 p.

> Capitalize only the initial word of titles.

4. Saunders, W. B., Work, D. M., Nikolaeva, S. V., Evolution of complexity in Paleozoic ammonoid sutures. Science. 1999; 286: 760–763.

5. Lewy, Z., The function of the ammonite fluted septal margins. Journal of Paleontology. 2002; 76: 63–69.

6. Daniel, T. L., Helmuth, B. S., Saunders, W. B., Ward, P. D., Septal complexity in ammonoid cephalopods increased mechanical risk and limited depth. Paleobiology. 1997; 23: 470–481.

> Use only initials for first and middle names; do not include URLs.

7. Saunders, W. B., The ammonoid suture problem: relationships between shell and septum thickness and suture complexity in Paleozoic ammonoids. Paleobiology. 1995; 21: 343–355.

8. McShea, D. W., The evolution of complexity without natural selection, a possible large-scale trend of the fourth kind. Paleobiology. 2005; 31: 146–156.

9. Garciaruiz, J. M., Checa, A. G., Rivas, P., Paleobiology. 1990; 16: 349–354.

10. T. M. Lutz, G. E. Boyajian, Fractal Geometry of ammonoid sutures. Paleobiology. 1995; 21: 329–342.

11. Checa, A. G., Fabrication and function of ammonite septa: comment on Lewy. Journal of Paleontology. 2003; 77: 790–791.

12. Lewy, Z., Reply to checa and to Hewitt and Westerman. Journal of Paleontology. 2003; 77: 796–798.

13. Perez-Claros, J. A., Allometric and fractal exponents indicate a connection between metabolism and complex septa in ammonites. Paleobiology. 2006; 31: 221–232.

14. Allen, E. G. New approaches to Fourier analysis of ammonoid sutures and other complex, open curves. Paleobiology. 2006; 32: 299–315.

4   Philosophy Essay

With Components of Pro-Con and Classification Reasoning

Student Name
Course and Instructor Name
Date

Plato's Ideal City-State: An Honorable but Naïve Notion

One of the most intriguing aspects of Plato's *Republic* is his idea of the ideal city-state, as presented through the voice of his mentor, Socrates. Socrates makes a compelling case for a city-state governed by "philosopher-kings" who hand down laws that curb the natural evils of man and establish a society where good can prevail. According to Socrates, this can be achieved through assigning noble guardians and a king to rule the city, and by allowing the citizens to find harmony and peace in performing the jobs for which they are most suited. However, while his city seeks a sort of cosmic balance, it can never stay in harmony with human nature, with its natural desire for honest expression and for the accumulation of wealth and power. Although some individuals could rise above these desires to achieve an ideal city the way Socrates imagined it, everyone would have to comply, which is not at all realistic.

In Book II, Socrates peoples his imaginary city with four types of men – the farmer, the house-builder, the weaver, and the leatherworker. All of these talents are necessary to society, and efficiency is achieved because each worker does the work for which he is best suited (61). By matching each man to his skills, each would perform his tasks excellently.

> First the Pro arguments are presented.

If an excellent farmer were forced to make his own clothes as well as farm, not only would he wear substandard clothes, but he would also jeopardize his harvest because he would be unable to spend all his time tending the fields, being forced to work inefficiently at a task for which he has little talent. With each man performing just one task, the city will need additional specialized workers, each contributing his own particular skill. In order for a farmer to plow his field he needs a plow and oxen. In order for there to be a plow and oxen, there must be a plow-maker and a person who raises oxen. In order for a clothes-maker to make

> The first body paragraph offers a classification of one group of city dwellers, the workers.

clothes, there must be a weaver. This list gets longer when one realizes that goods and services have to be traded in a market place, between cities, and overseas, requiring people to do the trading, the traveling, and the sailing, and maintaining the city's sanitation (62–63). With each man simply performing the job he does most beautifully and only doing as much as needs to be done, Socrates imagines his ideal city will be fruitful and healthy.

So far Socrates has addressed only the basic necessities of life. He has not accounted for "extraneous" jobs such as artists, writers, musicians, or actors. Socrates refers to these as

> The second body paragraph classifies a second group of city dwellers, the artists.

"luxuries" and argues that a city will become spoiled and corrupt with the inclusion of too many luxuries, just as a meal is ruined by too many deserts and too much wine. Socrates understands that eventually, the people will want daily luxuries such as sofas, perfumes, cakes, and art (64). This will require more workers, and servants, leading to increased population, such that the city would outgrow its land, and would have to

> Since the essay only refers to one work, only the page numbers is needed.

go to war against neighboring cities in order to obtain more land to feed the additional people. Thus the city will need a professional army to protect the city and to go to war for more land (65). Some luxuries Socrates permits, but he supplies his city with guardians to protect the citizens and city from unwholesome luxuries.

To defend the people from unwholesome desires, Socrates proposes education as the key to good citizenship. Logically, he begins with the education of the guardians. Socrates insists that the guardians be trained in the crucial arts of music and gymnastics, to strengthen their souls, convincing them to avoid the other arts, for indulging those luxuries could cause illness of the soul or body (69). Through this training, the guardians become temperate and wise, resistant to ambition and greed, for their characters would have been formed by experiencing only good ideas. The honorable luxuries of music and gymnastic would be the only luxuries allowed in the city. In addition, Socrates argues that only good stories, images, and songs would be told, because the good characters will serve as role models (77–78). For example, he would disallow stories of warriors fearing death or weeping for the death of a loved one because this might cause men to fear going to

> The third and fourth paragraphs discuss a third group of city dwellers, the guardians, or leaders.

battle. To instill courage, they should hear many stories of men going bravely to their deaths. Since warriors could only be depicted doing heroic deeds, much of the *Iliad* would have to be censored, since Achilles argues with his commanding officer, cries about losing his prize, and falls into a rage after his friend Patroclus dies. Socrates also outlaws tragedy and comedy, the "imitative" arts, for men might imitate the evils depicted in the theater (87–88). With regard to music, only that which inspires courage and noble deeds should be allowed, and the same goes for speeches (91–92). The guardians must be ever vigilant to allow only sanctioned poets, artists, musicians, and actors to perform the acceptable arts, al to maintain the city's healthy harmony.

Socrates mentions doctors and judges as special types of guardians (100–103). Doctors guard the body against harms, while judges guard the soul from injustices. Socrates believes that a bodily sickness occurs when something is out of harmony in the body, and that a man who performs evil deeds has something out of harmony in his soul. In order for a doctor to cure a sick body, he must learn about many different types of illnesses. Therefore, the doctor should become infected by many kinds of diseases himself in order to learn as much as he possibly can so that he may help others. Judges, however, should follow the opposite path. Socrates believes that judges should remain ignorant of injustices for as long as possible and only be shown justice. In this way, when exposed to injustice, the situation would not resonate with the contents of his just soul, making injustice easily identifiable.

Socrates sums up the three categories of worker metaphorically in terms of three metals. He says that the farmers and craftsmen have bronze in their souls, that the guardians and army have silver souls, and that the rulers have gold souls (109). A person is not placed in their position based on parentage, but on the composition of his soul. A child born to farmers does not have to be a farmer and could in fact be found to have a golden soul and so be placed in charge of the entire city.

> Now all of the city dwellers are reclassified, according to their type of soul.

With this means of identifying types of people, Socrates believes that his ideal republic can remain in complete harmony, and will thus be completely good (120).

However, Socrates ignores several aspects of human nature that would create havoc in his ideal republic. First, his strict regulations conflict with the human desire to express oneself. Socrates believes that his limited arts will satisfy the citizens, but artists by their nature always search for new forms of expression—just as Socrates has done in writing his Republic. History is filled with artists who innovate by rejecting or revising the art of their predecessors. This will happen in poetry, tragedy, music, and art, because it is part of human nature to be creative and to imitate as well as to distort reality,

> The essay shifts to discuss the failures of Plato's city-state—the Con arguments—from least to most important.

no matter how noble or evil it is. Socrates cannot eliminate all bad things from the populace, for there will always be a scorned lover, a man who flees the battle field, or a friend who dies before his time, and these events will find their way into the arts. The arts must represent evil as well as good, because both are part of human experience and should be cherished for what they are and what they teach.

By eliminating choice, Socrates courts disaster. Humans must choose moderation, and will resist it if it is forced upon them. Emotions must find expression. A man who cannot weep when his wife or children die, or who is not allowed to express love for his family and friends, will suppress his feelings, which, as psychology teaches, can creates undue stress and subconscious feelings that manifest themselves at undesirable times and in unwanted ways. Obviously Socrates did not have the foresight to understand all that modern psychology has to offer, but common sense suggests that we cannot simply will emotions into compliance.

Furthermore, his city will cannot survive as a closed society (63). It must trades with other cities, both over land and sea, which will result in an exchanges of ideas, skills, art, music, and literature. Such communication with other peoples would enrich the city's culture. Inevitably, the citizens in this city will see other cities allowing freedom of expression and demand it for themselves.

Perhaps the most glaring flaw in Socrates' conception of an ideal city-state relates to the natural human desire for wealth. He argues that if a person's education is pure, then there will be no need to regulate commerce, including contracts among merchants and between employees and employers (118). However, humans are naturally self-interested and will only trade and make contracts so long as it is personally advantageous. If the guardians of his city fail to recognize the reality of self-interest, they may not make laws to protect from one citizen taking advantage of another. The city needs laws to protect the people, not just an idealistic education.

Finally, Socrates assumes that given the right education, men will forget the desire for power. The governing system in this city is based on appointment of a ruler based on a series of tests and hardships (108). This allows anyone—no matter who his parents are—the chance to become a ruler. However, it will always be easier for a child from a wealthy to triumph than for a child from a poor laborer's family to triumph. It is unlikely that a child of a poor family could emerge from hardships to rise to the pinnacle of leadership. Furthermore, since power is a driving force in human nature, the guardians could become corrupt in their choice of leaders. All men desire power for themselves and for their children, so it is only natural that a guardian would assure that his own son would be selected as a potential guardian. Democracies are not immune to base human motivations, and no amount of quality education can eradicate the natural desire for power.

Socrates presents many innovative and honorable ideas that have inspired much good over the centuries. But he lived in a time when such ideas had never been tested in governments, so one can see why he is blind to the flaws in his system. If his ideas could be followed perfectly to the letter, as he argues they should, they might result in harmony and therefore good. However, people being who they are, this simply cannot

> The conclusion makes a concession (If his ideas could be followed perfectly) and comes to an efficient ending.

happen on as large a scale as would be necessary to create this city. Cities must be founded on realities and not ideals, which is why this particular beautiful ideal falls short.

Plato. *Plato Republic*. trans. Joe Sachs. Newburyport, Ma: Focus Publishing/R. Pullins Co., 2006.

5   Environmental Science Paper

CSE Style, with Components of Problem/Solution, Pro-Con, and Cause/Effect Analysis

Securing Food for Africa

Student Name

Environmental Strategies 245
Instructor Name
Date

Note: Longer essays require a separate cover page and division into sections.

Abstract

As the population grows and global warming reduces farmable land, food shortages have occurred across the world, but the worst conditions exist in Sub-Saharan Africa. Its food yields have stagnated while its population continues to burgeon. Conflicts over resources have led to violence, as in Ethiopia, Rwanda, Somalia and Sudan (Brown 2009, Mekonnen 2006). While other developing nations, such as India and China, increased their agricultural yields through agricultural reform during the Green Revolution of the 1940s-1970s, Sub-Saharan Africa has not increased its yield, while its population has grown. What lessons from the Green Revolution can help Africa catch up to other developing regions and securely provide its nations with nutritious food?

The abstract provides a brief summary of the topic.

Introduction: the Scope of the Food Security Problem in Africa

> The introduction explains why this topic matters.

According to the World Health Organization (WHO), 925 million people go hungry every year, and this number is growing by 79 million per year (Brown 2010; Welch et al. 1997). Africa accounts for more than ¼ of that number. The Food and Agriculture Organization of the United Nations (FAO) notes in its 2010 publication The State of Food Security in the World (SOFI) that twenty-two nations endure a state of protracted crisis where up to 37% of their population is hungry. These countries face a triple threat: depletion of natural resources, population exodus, and conflict (SOFI). Additionally, climate change has led to droughts, with the result that

> This essay uses the CSE Name-Date citation method. Author's last name and the date of publication are parenthetically cited. Include date to distinguish multiple works by one author.

food prices have soared (Rowe 2010 Jan). Because of global warming and excessive clearing there have been increasingly frequent and more devastating dust storms, too, which annually carry away three billion tons of topsoil from Africa (Brown 2004).

Among the countries burdened by hunger, Sub-Saharan African countries have the highest percentage of hungry people, and a disproportionally larger number of African countries have also succumbed to conflicts precipitated by competition over food sources. This results when farmers, following crop failure or cattle raiding, migrate from rural to urban locations where crowding can exacerbate ethnic differences between groups that had previously coexisted peacefully—when resources were not at a premium. And with one in six people already lacking access to safe drinking water as well as receding

> Much of this section contains Cause/Effect and Problem/Consequence reasoning.

water tables due to over-pumping, it has been predicted that most future wars in this century will be fought over water (Rowe 2010 Apr; Brown Plan B).

To complicate matters, as developing nations progress, their populations consume more meat and dairy products in place of grains and legumes. Since grains are the primary source of nutrition for feeding food animals, grain availability is reduced overall when it gets diverted to feed lots (Brown 2009). As the world population

> Claims are supported by statistics from reliable sources.

grows and as more and more people add meat and dairy to their diets, overall food supplies will have to increase by 70% to feed the world's 6.8 billion humans (Rowe 2010 Jan). Unless steps are taken soon to secure food resources for all countries, this goal cannot be met. Even though 60% of Africa's population engages in agriculture, Sub-Saharan African nations will especially need to focus on food security, as they are already behind the rest of the world in food production, (Versi 2008). In addition, Africa's over 75% Africa's farmland has been degraded through overproduction, overgrazing, and desertification (Versi 2008). With over a third of Africans malnourished already, Africa will need assistance to catch up.

Lessons Learned from the Green Revolution

The original Green Revolution took place during a thirty-year period between the 1940s and 1970s in India, China, Mexico, and elsewhere, where a combination of newly developed hybrid seeds, fertilizer, and pesticides resulted in higher crop yields. The Green Revolution (the name was a play on the Red—communist—Revolution) was a huge success in that it resulted in at

> This section covers background information.

least doubling the crop yields of rice and wheat in Southeast Asia, India, and China (Wu and Butz 2004). Farmers were able to purchase inexpensive fertilizers and pesticides to produce more crops per acre, using specialized hybrid plants designed to grow faster and larger. Ironically, though, the Green Revolution, while increasing crop production and thus creating greener agricultural fields, was not at all Green in the environmental sense. Instead, the significant increases in quantitative yield came at the cost of qualitative harms: loss of crop diversity, contamination of soil and waterways by pesticides and fertilizers, and soil depletion by overproduction and dust storms, as well as inefficient plant strains that, while growing faster and absorbing the targeting micronutrient of iron, at the same time failed to absorb other crucial micronutrients (Wu and Butz 2004; Welch et al. 1997). The triple combination of hybrid or genetically modified plants, fertilization, and pesticides made short-term gains but had devastating long-term costs.

> For more than two authors, list the first one and "et al," which means "and others."

For several reasons, Africa did not participate in the Green Revolution. Most of its nations lacked the infrastructure, planning, and research capability to do so, though it had some potential to undertake parts of it. For example, Africa has large deposits of phosphate, a key ingredient for fertilizer, but no facilities for turning it into fertilizer, and thus much of it was (and is) sold elsewhere; in the meantime, rising fertilizer prices have hampered African crop yields (Versi 2008). Without fertilizer, a vicious cycle occurs, in that once cropland soil is depleted, farmers clear forest to create new fields, thus exacerbating soil loss through erosion, since trees help keep soil in place (Rowe 2010 Jan, Versi 2008). The cost of pesticide also prohibits most African farmers from using it to improve yields, which has avoided some of the soil and waterway contamination experienced by the Green Revolution countries, however small a compensation that may be. Finally, the hybrid or genetically modified plants developed during the Green Revolution do not thrive in African soil. The thin topsoil and frequent drought conditions require a completely different kind of plant strain (Pinstrup-Andersen and Schioler 2001). New strains will have to be engineered to take advantage of regional soil and weather conditions, with the added concern to assure the micronutrient take-up that the other hybrids fail to absorb. The research to produce new strains of crop plants is expensive—often far beyond the reach of African resources (Brown 2009). Even if African researchers can produce the needed strains, the poorest of those farmers would not be able to afford buying them for every planting season, as biotech patents would require them to do (Wu and Butz 2004).

How Can Sub-Saharan Africa Undertake a Successful Green Revolution of its Own?

To feed its hungry, Africa must take the lessons learned from the Green Revolution and focus not just on increasing yield but also on producing the variety of important micronutrients that now are recognized as crucial to good health. Staples such as rice, wheat, and corn, even

This section assesses various solutions to the problem using Pro and Con and Problem/Solution analysis.

in greater quantities, do not provide the micronutrients of iron, zinc, iodine, vitamins A and C, riboflavin, selenium, copper, and other essentials to health (Welch, et al. 1997) In fact, focusing exclusively on the yield and iron content of three staples during the Green Revolution resulted in people reducing their intake of local fruits and vegetables that provide such micronutrients (Welch et al. 1997). In places, this led to stunted growth in children (Welch et al. 1997; Brown Plan B). Diversity in crops as well as in diet will go a long way to improve overall health (Welch et al. 1997). Educating farmers as well as the general public about nutrition is another key aspect of diversity of food options (Hussey 2009). However, since good nutrition comes from eating a diversity of foods, often the poor cannot afford to obtain the variety they need. So Africa must encourage home gardening and local farming of diverse foods and educate its population to seek nutrition from sources besides staple foods (Brown 2010). In the short term, governments may have to supplement nutritional sources through food aid, but the ultimate goal should be to develop self-sufficient local farming.

One of the most significant advances of the Green Revolution was the implementation of double or multiple cropping—planting and harvesting more than one crop in a given year. In Asia, this resulted in tripling the output of grain (Brown 2009). Since double cropping requires more water, planting shade trees can help to prevent water evaporation as well (Brown 2009). But even more important is the expansion of irrigation.

In Africa, improved water irrigation is a challenge. Already, 87% of fresh water goes to crop irrigation, yet only 20% of farmland is irrigated (Rowe 2010 Apr). Therefore, it is crucial to select the best of the new technologies in irrigation to make it possible to expand irrigation to more types of lands as well as to increase the effectiveness of irrigation using such methods as subsurface watering, which waters plant roots directly, thus reducing loss through evaporation (Rowe 2010 Apr). Systems need to be designed for local soil composition, humidity, and rainfall conditions (Brown 2009). In addition, some consideration worldwide will eventually need to be given to increasing the price of water, which is free in most of Africa and subsidized in the developed world; economically, this will lead to more efficient distribution and usage (Rowe 2010 Apr).

New techniques in general farm management can also play a large role. Initially, farmers need to be taught simple techniques such as using fertilizer, rotating crops, and planting in rows. In places where this has been done, it has taken only two years for farmers to produce a surplus (Beard 1997). At the same time, new technologies that enable precision fertilizer application can also increase efficiency. In the United States, farmers are using GPS systems to avoid wasteful overlapping when applying fertilizer by tractor, as well as new software that tracks yields by crop location, allowing farmers to target specific areas for more or less amounts of fertilizer (Little 2009). With fertilizer prices rising, efficiency is paramount. Since fertilizer can double yields, farmers who use it efficiently can produce significant surpluses, thus making it possible to invest in more fertilizer and more diverse crops, with compounding benefits.

The Green Revolution included experimentation with hybrid and genetically modified seeds, but it mostly focused on increasing the size of the plant. With more sophisticated plant engineering techniques, new seeds are being designed to utilize fertilizer more efficiently, resist insect damage, and to efficiently take up nutrients in local soil conditions (Little 2010). For Sub-Saharan Africa to benefit the most from such scientific advancements, local scientists need to receive the necessary training to breed new strains of seeds themselves. This will avoid the current problem of biotech patents that has priced new strains beyond the reach of African farmers (Wu and Butz 2004).

Once some of these measures begin to produce results, both general health and the economy will get a boost which leads to greater prosperity in general. Farmers will have surpluses of produce and livestock to sell, but this will create another need: in order for food producers to sell their excess crops and livestock, roads need to be built so give access to markets (Beard 1997). Governments will have to invest in transportation avenues to provide access to markets. This investment is just part of the larger infrastructure changes that will become necessary.

In addition to improving transportation, governments need to tune up legal codes to ensure that property rights are secure and to facilitate the availability of bank

More Cause/Consequence analysis.

loans for farm expansion, procuring improved seeds, and for installing improved irrigation systems(Wu and Butz 2004). Protective legislation must be passed to prevent other countries from buying Sub-Saharan African land in order to expand their own food growing capacity. Several countries (eg., South Korea, China, Saudi Arabia) that have run out of agricultural land have already purchased large swaths of territory in other countries, such as Kazakhstan, Ethiopia, and Sudan (Brown 2009; Rowe 2010 Jan). Governments must also prevent corruption from diverting aid and supplies from agricultural endeavors; Amartya Sen and others have shown that some of the famines that have occurred during times of drought could have been prevented had the government stepped in and distributed some of its (often ample) funds to provide food, aid, and emergency supplies instead of hoarding donations and selling them at extortionist prices (Rowe 2010 Jan). If the government does not play its part, the African Green Revolution could fail before it gets a running start.

On the international level, rethinking aid can also contribute to food security in Africa. Currently, many African nations have come to depend on aid to solve their economic problems, creating aid dependency (Moye). Investing in their own economies and their own food-producing capacity will mean that aid can be targeted at specific needs, such as wiping out malaria and researching better crop strains. Governments will have to address corruption as well as distribution of goods and services as well as also education to ensure a successful path to food independence. In this respect, the international community can play a role in strongly encouraging Sub-Saharan African nations to begin to take responsibility for their own food security.

Signs of Progress

In June, 2006, at a summit on fertilizers, the African Union (AU) made a serious commitment to food security when they launched the African Green Revolution (Versi 2008). Branching beyond just the need to develop organic fertilizers and fertilizers to address specific micronutrients, the summit recognized the need to plan for investment and subsidies, transportation expansion, and retail markets (Versi 2008). While not much progress has been made as of yet, the time is ripe to act on these promises and seek to implement the commitments made at the summit.

Conclusion

Sub-Saharan Africa has lagged behind other nations in establishing the groundwork to achieve food security. However, the technological gains made elsewhere can provide a fast track to success, if governments prepare wisely and local farmers and livestock producers are given

> The reader should be able to predict what the Conclusion will say, as the whole essay has explained it.

the training, money, and legal assistance they need to implement new procedures and expand their producible lands.

References

Beard, A. 1997 Aug 7. Hopes rise that Africa will soon feed itself. The Washington Times P. 12.

> List authors alphabetically. List multiple works by one author in date order. Note that here there are three authors with the last name of Brown.

Brown, L. R. 2010 Jan–Feb. How to feed 8 billion people: record grain shortages are threatening global food security in the immediate future. The Futurist. P. 44.

Brown, L. 2009. Plan B 4.0: Mobilizing to Save Civilization. New York, NY: W. W. Norton & Co. 384 p.

Brown, P. 2004 Aug 20. 4x4s replace the desert camel and whip up a worldwide dust storm. Guardian London.

Hussey, H. 2009 Jan–Feb. No water, no peace: beyond the ethnic battle in Darfur. The Humanist. P. 69.

> For books, list the number of total pages at the end. For journals, the starting page. This is unique to CSE citation.

Iqbal, B. A., Mathur, N. 2009. Food in crisis: Badar Alam Iqbal and Navin Mathur analyse different facets of the growing world food crisis and suggest strategies for addressing the crisis. New Zealand Internat. Review 34(1).

Little, A. 2009. Power trip: the story of America's love affair with energy. New York, NY: Harper Perennnial. 446 p.

Mekonnen, M. 2006 Sept. Drought, famine, and conflict: case from the Horn of Africa. Beyond Intractability [Internet]. [cited 201 December 21]. Available from: www.beyondintractability.org

Moye, D. 2009. Dead aid: why aid is not working and how there is a better way for Africa. New York, NY: Farrar, Straus, and Giroux, 188 p.

Pinstrup-Andersen P, Schioler, E. 2001. Seeds of Contention. Baltimore: The Johns Hopkins University Press. 176 p.

Rowe, M. 2010 Jan. Feed the world. Geographical 82. [Internet]. [cited 2010 Dec 5]. Available from: http://www.questiaschool.com/read/5040173616? title=Feed%20the%20World

Rowe, M. 2010 Apr. A watershed moment. Geographical 82. [Internet].[cited 2010 Dec 5]. Available from: http://www.questiaschool.com/read/5044264197? title=A%20Watershed%20Moment

Versi, A. 2008 June. Why Africa Needs a Green Revolution. African Business. [Internet] [cited 2010 Dec 14]. Available from: http://www.questiaschool.com/ PM.qst?a=o&d=5028047419#

Versi, A. 2010 Dec. Taking the first steps: while the rest of the world has availed itself of scientific advances to triple its food production, Africa's output is stagnating. It imports more food than it grows and three quarters of its farmland is degraded. But, as Anver Versi Reports, the first step has been taken in launching the continent's Green Revolution. African Business. [Internet]. [cited 2010 Dec 21]. Available from: http://www.questiaschool.com/read/5018738459

Welch, R. M., Combs, G. F., & Duxbury, J. M. 1997 Fall. Toward a "Greener" Revolution. Issues in Science and Technology. [Internet]. [cited 2010 Dec 12]. Available from: http://www.questiaschool.com/PM.qst?a=o&d=5000570898

Wu, F., Butz, W. 2004. The future of genetically modified crops: lessons from the green revolution. Santa Monica, Ca: Rand, 84 p.

CMS (Chicago Manual of Style) Citation, with Cause-Effect Analysis

Course and Instructor Name
Date

The Charismatic Leadership of Fidel Castro

Student Name

While Castro rose to power on a platform of economic and social change, his demands were not in keeping with the real needs of the Cubans. In fact, Cuba, just before Fidel Castro's revolution of 1958, was slowly but measurably gaining economic and social progress. Nevertheless, Castro convinced the population that only a revolution would set Cuba free from the imperialist clutches of the United States and rectify the poverty experienced by portions of the working force. He succeeded, not because of a perceived need for violent change, but because he made a convincing case for it. It was not the necessity for revolution that transformed Cuba from a thriving island economy to the oppressed regime that it now is; it was the population's vulnerability to Castro's charismatic leadership.

> The essay starts with a strong, controversial thesis (It was not the necessity...) that the essay will prove.

The economic state in Batista's Cuba did not necessitate a revolution. Although Castro criticized aspects of Cuba's economy under Batista, if anything, Cuba was heading towards a free market economy. In 1957 Cuba had the highest per capita income among all countries in the wet tropical zone and higher real wages than any country in the Western Hemisphere excluding the U.S. and

> Each paragraph assesses a different cause for the Cuban revolution. The topic sentence announces the cause being analyzed.

Canada. According to Boris Goldenberg, "Among the twenty Latin American republics, Cuba ranked fifth in annual income per capita, third in persons not employed in agriculture, third or fourth in life expectancy, first in railroad construction and possession of television sets, second in energy consumption, fourth in the production of doctors per thousand inhabitants" (qtd in Wolf[1]). Not only was the Cuban economy viable and serviceable for many of the Cuban people, Cuba was beginning to diversify its industries to provide long-term economic stability. While sugar made up 80% of Cuba's exports in 1952, "Cuba's new development strategy in the 1950s aimed at reducing the economy's dependence on its traditional export staple while stimulating industrial and agricultural diversification. These measures, though understandably new and fragile, spanned the economy, from tourism, to the production of cement, rubber tires, and chemical fertilizer."[2] With the diversification of agriculture and industry, the Cuban stage was set for a thriving middle class to develop. However, most Cubans were unaware of their island's economic potential. Large parts of the population worked in the sugar industry, with its low wages and seasonal job shortages. These workers believed Castro's claim that economic changes were needed. There is always a lag between economic reality and public opinion about it, and Castro was able to take advantage of the Cubans' naiveté about their economic prospects. Castro blamed the worker's problems on the imperialist relationship with the United States. But, was Castro correct in saying that the level of United States involvement in the Cuban economy was detrimental?

> When citing a source you found in another source, say "qtd in" for "quoted in."

> Question used as a transitional sentence.

The United States had been a major player in the Cuban economy since the 1898 revolution that the United States assisted. Yes, it was an imperialistic relationship. By 1959, "the United States accounted for

---

1 Eric Wolf, *Peasant Wars of the Twentieth Century* (New York, NY: Harper & Row, 1969), 259.
2 Eric N. Baklanoff, "Cuba before Fidel," *Latin Business Chronicle.* (February 25, 2008), http://www.latinbusinesschronicle.com.

74 percent of Cuban export sales and supplied 65 percent of its imports."[3] Next to Brazil, Cuba was the most important Latin American source of agricultural imports of the United States. And this was not all. "In addition, American interests dominated many key activities, including telephone and electric light and power companies, which operated in an atmosphere of general public hostility. A major railroad system serving the eastern half of the island was American-controlled"[4] The United States had built infrastructure in the backwards island in order to conduct its business there. However, by doing so, as often happens in imperialist relationships, this investment in infrastructure created a starting point for future growth in the colonial economy. Unfortunately, though, Cuba did not realize how much potential it had.

This potential lay in the very success of U.S. enterprise, which actually resulted in making opportunities for Cuban entrepreneurs. Those Cubans who worked for Americans saved their wages and built up personal capital in order to start their own businesses. Eventually, "Cuban capital controlled three-fourths of the sugar mills; and these, in turn, accounted for 62 percent of the island's sugar production in 1958."[5] Trade with the U.S. was in many ways a positive situation for Cuba, for it created the possibility for growth in a new middle class of entrepreneurs who could perpetuate the process of putting Cuban business into Cuban hands. In other words, the impact of U.S. involvement had more than just a profitable effect on the U.S.; it also sparked important growth in the Cuban middle class.

> Notice how the topic sentences together with the thesis statement make up a clear outline of the essay.

Nor was the Cuban revolution driven by social issues. At the time that Castro began making moves towards revolution, from 1955 through 1958, Cuba was enjoying relative socio-economic success as compared with other Latin American nations; "Cuba ranked third in Latin America on a per capita basis in daily calorie consumption, steel consumption, paper consumption and radios per 1,000 persons. In 1959, Cuba had one million radios and the highest ratio of television

---

3 Jorge I. Dominguez, *Cuba: Order and Revolution* (Boston, MA: Belknap Press, 1979), 149.

4 Philip W. Bonsal, "Cuba, Castro, and the United States," *Foreign Affairs* 45 no. 2 (1967): 265, http://www.jstor.org/stable/20039231 (accessed January 2, 2010).

5 Baklanoff, "Cuba before Fidel."

sets per 1,000 inhabitants."[6] This indicates a fairly good standard of living for a significant portion of Cuba's population. While it was true that a gap existed between the rich and the working poor, the socio-economic conditions in Cuba were not deplorable for the average Cuban. However, despite this measure of socio-economic success, certain social factors were passively simmering in Cuba before Castro, making the nation arguably ripe for revolution.

Life in Batista's Cuba was not ideal. One problem was the intermittent migration of farmers and rural workers to urban areas and cities during the ebbs and flows of the sugar harvest cycle. Workers who migrate to the city can become "transmitter[s] of urban unrest and political ideas" (qtd in Crahan[7]). This situation was fairly unique to Cuba. In the 1950s, Cuba developed industrially and the urban areas began to advance. Had the large population of rural proletariat and rural workers remained strictly rural, unrest likely would not have occurred at all, as agricultural-based peasants tend not to resort to revolution. As Crahan and Smith explain "it is no simple task to cultivate a popular following among workers or peasants."[8] In addition to the difficulty of pulling together rural workers, the population did not have the courage to challenge the ruthless dictatorial rule of Batista, who was known for his brutal suppression of any opposition. But as the rural workers traveled between their rural homes and urban areas, their eyes were opened to the growth and potential that was available to the urban populations. They developed an appetite for goods, an understanding of fair wages, and they made connections with other disaffected workers. They were not what Marx once dismissed as a "the lumpen proletariat"— uneducated, unmotivated, and immobile. As Castro understood, they were quite mobile and ready to hear his revolutionary message. With the already unique situation of the rural population's exposure to an urban lifestyle, Castro could exploit their new interest desires. Cuba's proletariat was ready to hear and comprehend messages of liberation. All that was missing was a charismatic leader to serve as the catalyst.

Batista had alienated many of his people through his sadistic regime and rampant corruption, where: "the number of murders by the Batista

---

6 Ibid.

7 Margaret E. Crahan, and Peter H. Smith, "The State of Revolution," in *Americas: New Interpretive Essays*, edited by Alfred Stepan (New York, NY: Oxford University Press, 1992), 87.

8 Ibid., 71.

security establishment during those bitter years [1952–1959] created thousands of deep hatreds."[9] In addition, by the time Castro and Che Guevara began to rally for

> Quoted material is seamlessly blended into the essay writer's own sentence.

revolution, there was already a "lack of faith in the political institutions."[10] So while socio-economic factors did not inspire a worker-led revolution, the workers were responsive to a leader who captured their attention by essentially "'parachuting' a rebel group into the Cuban situation" and starting a revolution.[11] Castro exuded a romantic spirit and a captivating willingness to challenge authority. As Castro drew attention to the glaring flaws of the incumbent leader, his claims for revolutionary change brought "support for the new regime [that] was widespread throughout Cuban society."[12] Castro made use of Cuba's "extensive television system and the mass rallies which on occasion [drew] as many as one million of Cuba's seven million inhabitants into the plaza of Havana" bringing his message to "almost 100 per cent of the population."[13] Castro was one of the first third-world leaders to make use of modern media to consolidate his power:

> Quoted passages over three lines long are indented and single spaced.

> Castro spoke practically every week on television, and was followed in his travels by representatives of all the media. His speeches were often made without warning, and lasted for many hours, upsetting the usual schedule of programs. Those in power were constantly in the news and the country was being rocked by the ongoing changes: the Rent Laws, the Agrarian Reform, the Tax Reform, the military trials of those accused of committing genocide during the Batista regime; the efforts of the various revolutionary organizations.[14]

---

9 Bonsal, "Cuba, Castro, and the United States," 265.

10 Nelson Amaro Victoria, "Mass and Class in the Origins of the Cuban Revolution," *Studies in Comparative International Development* 4, no. 10 (1968): 236, http://www.springerlink.com/content/pu078551x74k85q7/ (accessed December 19, 2009).

11 Wolf, *Peasant Wars*, 269.

12 Bonsal, "Cuba, Castro, and the United States," 266.

13 Richard R. Fagen, "Charismatic Authority and the Leadership of Fidel Castro," *The Western Political Quarterly* 18, no. 2, Part 1 (1965): 279, http://www.jstor.org/stable/444996 (accessed January. 2, 2010).

14 Victoria, "Mass and Class in the Origins of the Cuban Revolution," 231.

Compared to the brutal regime then in power, Castro "gained sympathies as a kind of Robin Hood," fighting the good fight against the evil dictator.[15] Through his charismatic behavior and speeches, Castro managed to convince the people that revolution was necessary and that he was the man to make it happen—and he became the people's hero. In their mountain hideaway, Castro's guerrilla band sniped at corrupt government officials while broadcasting messages of solidarity with exploited workers. He paid local farmers to feed his troops, which earned their support, and he got "financial support and tactical assistance for the rebellion...from middle- and upper-class Cubans."[16] Castro's managed to recruit 1,200–1,500 followers, and that turned out to be all that he needed to topple Batista's corrupt and weak government.

Castro also did everything in his power to appear a man of the people. He promised jobs for everyone and lowered prices for workers in "People's Shops...which offered merchandise to the peasants at practically cost price."[17] In addition, "The Prime Minister himself took walks in [impoverished] zones, and it was rumored that he carried a checkbook and would distribute checks then and there, according to the needs of the various zones."[18] Castro's personality and nationalistic idealism captured the hearts of the Cuban population. Castro also exploited the Cubans' resentment of the imperialistic role of the United States in the Cuban economy. Castro execrated "'Yankee Imperialism'" and [criticized] the old social classes which had reigned over Cuba."[19] Cubans "welcomed actions aimed at reducing American influence in the island as a reassertion of Cuban nationalism."[20] Even though it was an economically risky idea, Castro insisted on completely expelling the United States from the Cuban economy. In retrospect, this move was not the best strategy. Had Castro managed to negotiate a better relationship with the U.S. instead of nationalizing every industry in which the U.S. held ownership, Cuba might have continued its upward economic trend and that would have led to improved social conditions. However, Castro was blinded by his own popularity. Castro felt that he had to continue to play David to the U.S. Goliath to maintain his political authority at home.

---

15 Wolf, *Peasant Wars of the Twentieth Century*, 271. 231.
16 Crahan and Smith, "The State of Revolution," 89.
17 Victoria, "Mass and Class in the Origins of the Cuban Revolution," 231.
18 Ibid.
19 Ibid., 235.
20 Bonsal, "Cuba, Castro, and the United States," 266.

So this bearded idealist in quest of social justice came to epitomize Cuban nationalistic idealism in just the form that Cubans wanted to see in their political figurehead. However, "Castro was far more than [just] an adventurer or a guerrilla leader...he was perhaps the greatest demagogue ever to have appeared anywhere in Latin America. He had a power to persuade with words quite independent of the intrinsic worth of the particular notions he might be advancing at the moment...ideas [were] for Castro little more than servants of his lust for power."[21] While the people were convinced of his dedication to them, he was actually building his own personal dynasty. His ego proved to be the undoing of Cuba, and the making of his long-lived autocracy.

Economically and socially Cuba could have made respectable progress under the United States' continued influence, but Fidel Castro's charismatic leadership style and political ego propelled Cuba to follow him along a path that led to a rupture with the United States and the eventual decline of economic and social conditions in Cuba. He had a driving need to consolidate an authoritarian regime instead of a more inclusive, democratic new Cuba. Cuba's economy floated briefly after he took power, only to crash in the early 1960s. The subsequent improvements in social equity hardly outweigh the oppressive lack of human rights and the extensive poverty that Castro's regime has brought to Cuba. The inhabitants of this island still seem both mesmerized and repelled by this leader's charismatic influence.

Bibliography

Baklanoff, Eric N. "Cuba Before Fidel." *Latin Business Chronicle,* February 25, 2008, http://www.latinbusinesschronicle.com

Bonsal, Philip W. "Cuba, Castro, and the United States." *Foreign Affairs* 45, no.2 (1967): 260–276. http://www.jstor.org/stable/20039231 (accessed January 2, 2010).

Crahan, Margaret E., and Peter H. Smith. "The State of Revolution." In *Americas: New Interpretive Essays,* edited by Alfred Stepan, 79–108. New York: Oxford University Press, 1992.

CMS formatted bibliography. Note that CMS style requires a URL for online sources as well as the date accessed. Many other systems do not require this information.

---

21 Ibid, 266-67.

Dominguez, Jorge I. *Cuba: Order and Revolution.* Boston: Belknap Press, 1979.

Fagen, Richard R. "Charismatic Authority and the Leadership of Fidel Castro." *The Western Political Quarterly* 18.2, Part 1 (1965): 275–284. http://www.jstor.org/ stable/444996 (accessed January. 2, 2010).

Victoria, Nelson Amaro. "Mass and Class in the Origins of the Cuban Revolution." *Studies in Comparative International Development* 4, no.10 (October, 1968): 223–238. http://www.springerlink.com/content/pu078551x74k85q7/ (accessed December 19, 2009).

Wolf, Eric. *Peasant Wars of the Twentieth Century.* New York: Harper & Row, 1969.

CMS bibliography entries are not indented.

INDEX